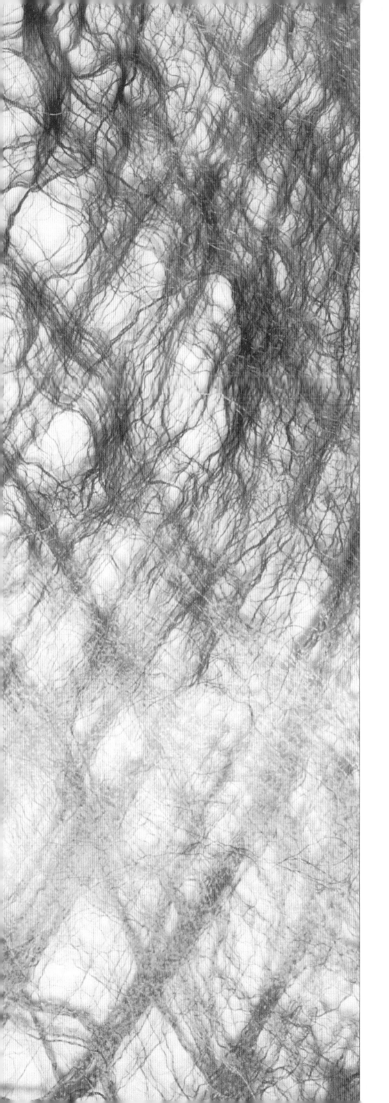

Sil... ap...

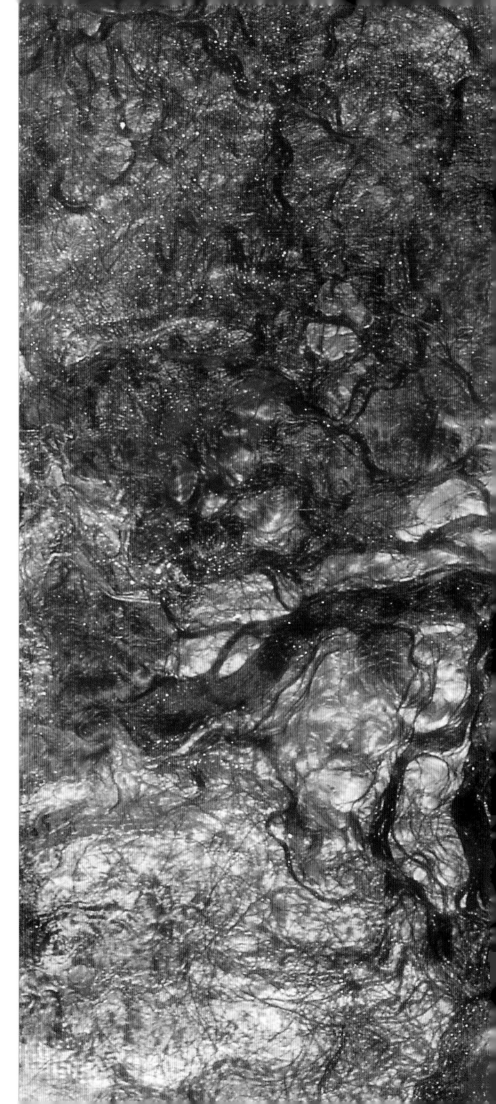

For Dave, Kate, Nic and Ben,
more precious to me than words can tell,
and for Hilda, Fred and Violet whose
love and support I hope, one day,
to deserve.

I am grateful to Niki Brown, Maggie Grey
and Diane Reade for the loan of their
inspirational pieces, and to Iain Stuart for
allowing the use of photographs as
credited. I acknowledge a debt of
gratitude to the many talented artists and
teachers who have, over the years,
shared freely of their time and skills. Pre-
eminent among them is Val Maden,
whose genorosity and creativity led me
to believe that I had something
worthwhile to say. The imperfections in
the saying are, as ever, my own.

Kath Russon

This colourful sheet of paper started with
a base layer of hand-dyed, degummed
silk filament fibres. I overlaid this with
clumps of hand-dyed kid mohair to
create blocks of solid colour. Finally, I
added a top layer of distorted raw silk
filament, hand-dyed in complementary
colours to create balance, as well as
movement, in the finished sheet.

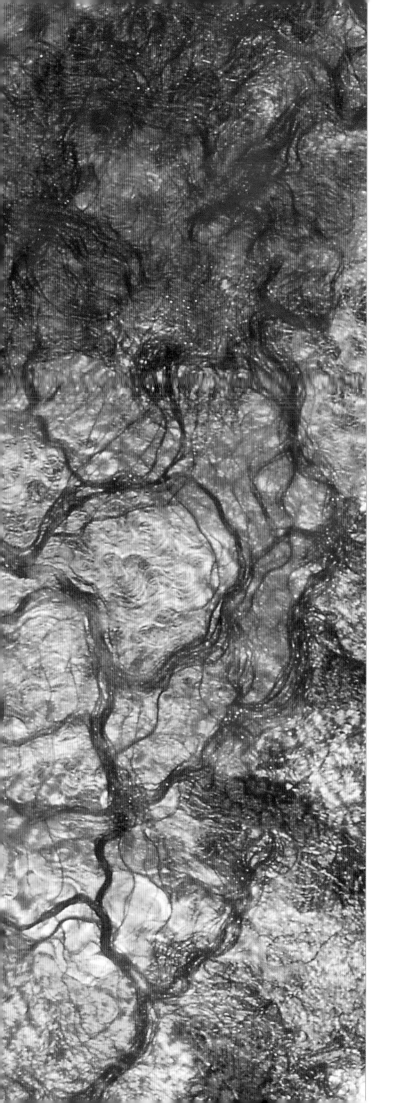

Handmade
Silk Paper

Kath Russon

SEARCH PRESS

First published in Great Britain 1999

Reprinted 2001
Search Press Limited
Wellwood, North Farm Road,
Tunbridge Wells, Kent TN2 3DR

Text copyright © Kath Russon 1999

Photographs copyright © Search Press Ltd. 1999, except
those on pages 18, 33 (bottom), 85 (top right and bottom,
which are by Iain Stuart, copyright © Iain Stuart 1999

Design copyright © Search Press Ltd. 1999

ISBN 0 85532 893 2

Suppliers
If you have any difficulty in obtaining any of the materials
and equipment mentioned in this book, then please write
to the publishers, at the above address, for a current list of
stockists, which includes firms who operate a mail-order
service.

Publisher's note
All the step-by-step photographs in this book feature the
author, Kath Russon, demonstrating how to make silk
papers. No models have been used.

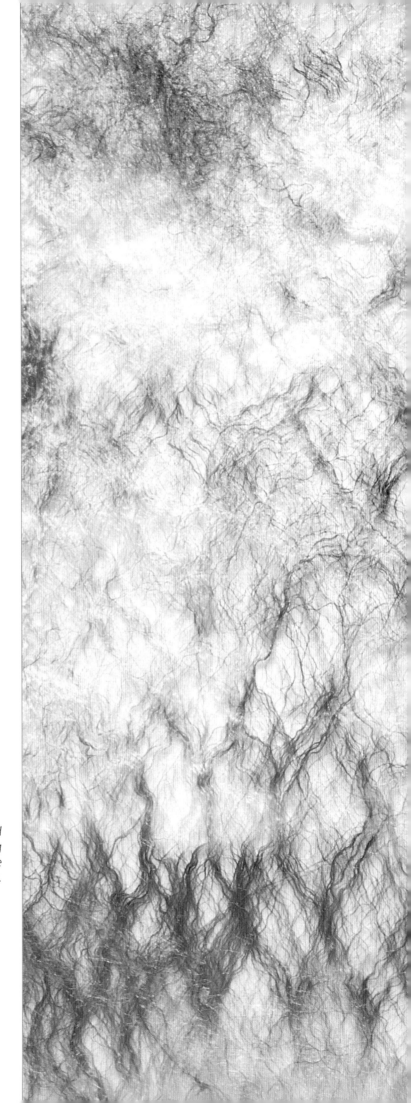

*Fine denier, hand-dyed, degummed hanked
filaments, stretched evenly across the felting
net as a single layer, produce the delicate
lacy effect of this paper.*

Colour separation by P&W Graphics, Singapore
Printed in Spain by A. G. Elkar, S. Coop. 48180 Loiu (Bizkaia)

Contents

Introduction

Paper is such an ordinary thing. We use it every day, usually without thinking about it. Silk, on the other hand, has always had an aura of mystery about it; it is extraordinary. Its lustre stops you in your tracks and makes you long to touch it. Imagine, then, making something as ordinary as paper out of something as extraordinary as silk.

There is nothing new about silk papermaking. Whilst paper as we know it is thought to have been invented by Cai Lunn, a Chinese eunuch in the court of Han Emperor Wu Di in the year 105AD, silk had been used long before this to record events for posterity. Apparently, by the second century BC it was widely used in China for official letters and documents. However, it was very expensive, so a method was developed by which old silk rags could be pulped; the resulting mixture, thinly spread on a frame, produced a material which could justifiably be termed silk paper.

For this stunning sheet of paper, layers of silk handkerchiefs have been separated then placed, unstretched as solid blocks of colour, on top of a muslin base. The resultant paper can be floppy or rigid, depending on the strength of the felting paste. This kind of paper is particularly prized by book artists since they can customise the colour, texture and weight of the paper.

In the course of this book, we shall try to copy the Chinese ancients in producing paper, in our case, not from pulp, but from actual silk fibres which are now available in a variety of formats, either undyed or dyed. The process of silk papermaking could not be simpler; you need no special tools or equipment and the process takes minutes rather than hours. Those of you who have tried feltmaking will recognise the preparation of fibres, but rejoice in the lack of rubbing and scrubbing, since an adhesive obviates the need to apply heat and friction to the fibres. The step-by-step instructions mean it is impossible to fail; the projects are attainable by papermakers of all ages and abilities, including those who have never thought of papermaking before.

There are all sorts of reasons why you might want to try making silk paper. You can paint on it, stitch into it, mould it, collage it and bead it; you can wax it, gild it, laminate it and even wear it. Silk paper can be also be made into three-dimensional bowls, boxes, masks and lampshades, bookcovers and multimedia collages, each one a unique work of art.

Embroiderers can quickly create a setting that is exactly the right colour and weight for their proposed stitches.

Silk and other fibres, once made into paper, can be moulded into bowls and vessels that are light and lustrous, yet surprisingly strong. By using single layers of fibre, the articles are completed in no time at all.

If you need to combine textures and colours into a multimedia backcloth that can be customised at all stages of its development, this papermaking technique can also be applied to

fibres other than silk. Equally, you might like to explore the many different kinds of silk fibres that are available, some of which you may not have thought of using before.

If you yearn to stand out from the crowd, you have only to turn the page; I guarantee your paper will never be ordinary again!

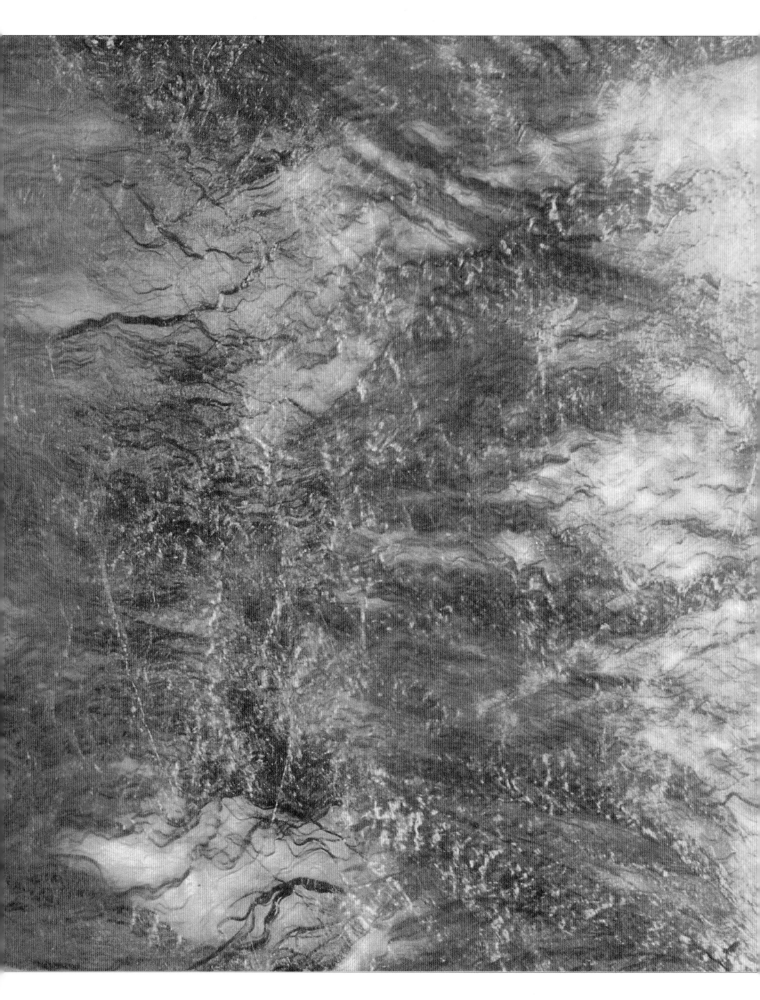

Materials and equipment

In this chapter I describe the materials and equipment used in all the projects in this book.

First, I discuss the raw materials that can be used to make paper – the various types of silk and other natural fibres that are available. I also include details of decorative materials that can be added to the fibres before felting.

Next, I introduce the equipment you need to dye your raw materials so that you can create some stunningly coloured papers.

Finally, I show you the equipment you will use to make your paper.

This paper is made from hand-dyed silk tops using the long-grain technique shown on page 42. The surface ripples are achieved by slightly distorting the grain of the silk as it is laid on the net. This sheet is a good example of space dyeing using a turkey baster (see page 26). Bands of colour have been carefully applied in repeating rows along the length of the silk brick. I used lemon, gold, caramel and apple green.

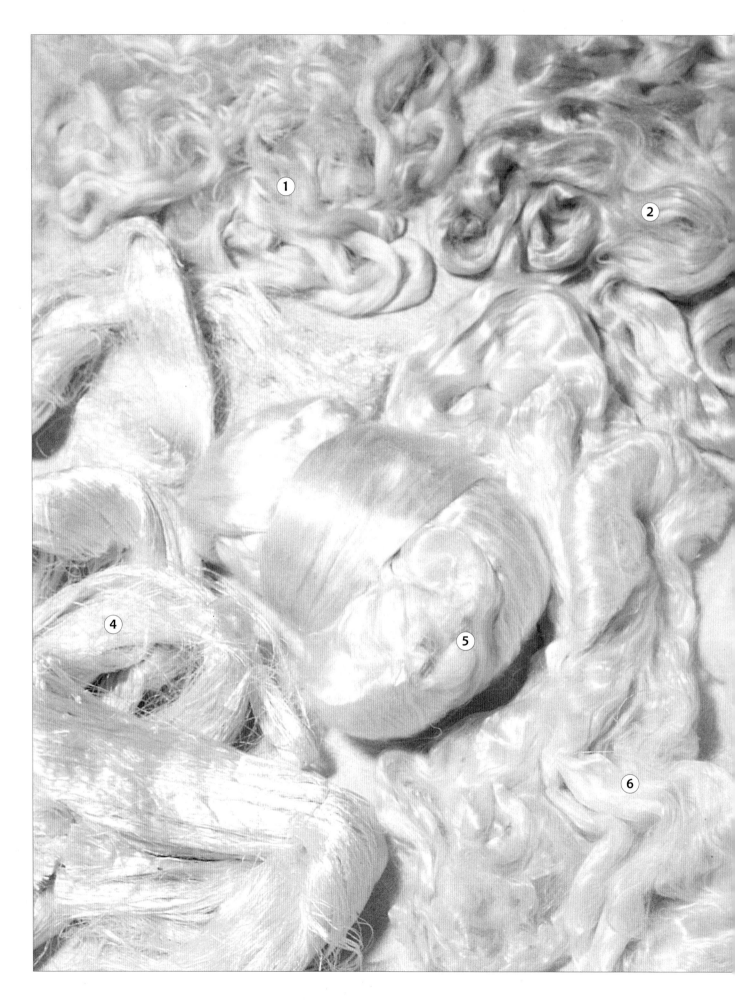

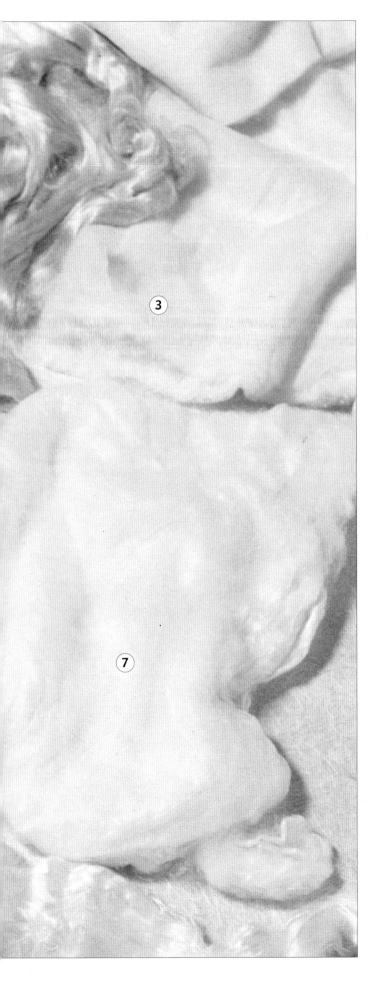

SILK FIBRES

Silk fibre starts life as a liquid produced by the silk worm, which is not really a worm at all, but a species of caterpillar grub. As you probably know, the silk worm spins a cocoon around itself prior to hatching. It extrudes fine strands of liquid protein coated with sericin (gum), which it flings into the air in a figure-of-eight pattern, rather like a cowboy trying to lasso his horse. These strands harden on exposure to air and settle back around the worm's body to form the protective cocoon. It is these cocoons that are used to produce the fibre we know as silk.

Silk worms can be farmed or found in the wild. Farmed worms are fed on specially grown and gathered mulberry leaves, and their cocoons have bright white fibres which are sold as mulberry silk. On the other hand, wild silk worms have a very varied diet, often including oak leaves. The tannin in the leaves passes through the system and produces cocoons with fibres that range in colour from pale champagne to strong tea. Wild silk is sold as tussah silk. Although both the lustre and staple length of tussah silk are thought to be inferior to that of mulberry silk, for our purposes tussah silk provides a delicate, natural contrast to its creamier cousin.

The cocoons are initially heated to kill the worm and then soaked in a warm alkali bath to release some of the sericin. Next, the long outer fibres of the cocoon are unravelled, several cocoons at a time, into a continuous filament referred to as reeled silk.

Reeled silk is turned into hanked continuous lengths of filament which are used by commercial spinners as their source material. These **hanked filaments** are also available to papermakers, usually as raw silk (i.e. still containing sericin), but it is possible to buy degummed hanked filaments. In this case, the heating process will have caused them to become regularly entwined along their length in a sort of diamond grid.

Some of the different types of silk fibres used
to make the papers featured in this book:
1. Throwster's waste
2. Tussah silk slivers
3. Silk wadding
4. Degummed hanked filaments
5. Silk 'brick'
6. Silk tops
7. Mawata caps

Yet another mysterious term you might come across is **throwster's waste**. This describes short, stranded filaments of silk that have passed through the spinner's (throwster's) machine. Discarded remnants are sold, usually in their raw (gummy) state as delicate tendrils of filament.

When reeled silk is carded it becomes soft and fluffy, like lustrous cotton wool, and this is termed **silk tops**. The greater the staple length and shine, the more expensive and prized is the fibre. Silk tops are sold in long rolled-up 'scarves' known as **silk bricks** or as long narrow lengths known as **silk slivers**.

Silk can be carded with other fibres, for example linen or merino wool, to produce **silk blends**. The joy for the papermaker is that if dye is applied, it is selectively taken up by each kind of fibre, thus producing a 'marbled' raw material from which to make unusual papers.

The shorter, inner fibres of the cocoon are processed into a matted form called **silk wadding** which is used primarily for insulation purposes. By-products from this process are often stretched over a bell-shaped former to make a 'bonnet' consisting of several individual fine layers of matted fibre. Each bonnet is called a **mawata cap**. Alternatively, you might be offered a **silk handkerchief**, which is a similar collection of delicate fibrous layers arranged in a flat wedge rather than a cap.

The innermost remains of the cocoon, containing the most sericin and having the shortest staple length are similarly processed, but are usually sold in a raw, sticky, shapeless mass known as carded cocoon strippings or **gummy silk**.

Silk noils also originate from the inner parts of the silkworm's cocoon, but in papermaking terms, they behave much more like raw cotton or silk blends.

OTHER FIBRES

The method of making paper from silk fibres described in this book can equally be applied to other kinds of fibre, including some kinds of processed fibres, such as cotton wool. As with silk, the format of the fibres will influence the way they are handled in the actual papermaking process.

All of these fibres can be used either dyed or undyed. Some of them are rather coarse, so you may find that you need a stronger concentration of paste. Alternatively, exploit the linear quality of these slivers to produce striped or woven papers.

As well as making interesting papers in their own right, natural fibres can also be used as a foundation for more delicate silk ones, to support them in a three-dimensional installation, perhaps.

Raw cotton has matted fibres and behaves much like silk tops. It is creamy white in colour and often contains seeds which enhance the texture of the resulting paper.

Sisal is the raw material used to make rope, matting and some strings. It has stranded fibres which are best handled like throwster's waste. Sisal is extremely strong and comes in very long lengths, so is suitable both for delicate papers or for large three-dimensional applications.

Jute can be bought as **raw jute** or as **crimped jute slivers**, which are reminiscent of permed hair! Softer than sisal, jute can be used either to make open, natural papers, or more often as a base support for other, luxury fibres. Treat as throwster's waste.

Flax is available as natural, bleached or dyed fibres. It is the source of linen cloth. It is immensely strong, yet softer and less coarse than sisal or jute. Again, treat as throwster's waste.

Ramie derives from the nettle plant. It resembles bleached flax but it has a wonderful lustre that linen fibre lacks. Unfortunately it is a difficult fibre to source these days.

Cotton wool can also be peeled into layers in the same way as silk wadding. For the beginner, cotton wool is an inexpensive alternative to its silken counterpart.

Opposite
Some of the other fibres that can used for making paper.
 1. Tussah silk noils
 2. Cotton wool
 3. Sisal
 4. Crimped jute
 5. Silk/Merino blend
 6. Raw cotton
 7. Gummy silk
 8. Silk/linen blend
 9. Raw jute
10. Flax

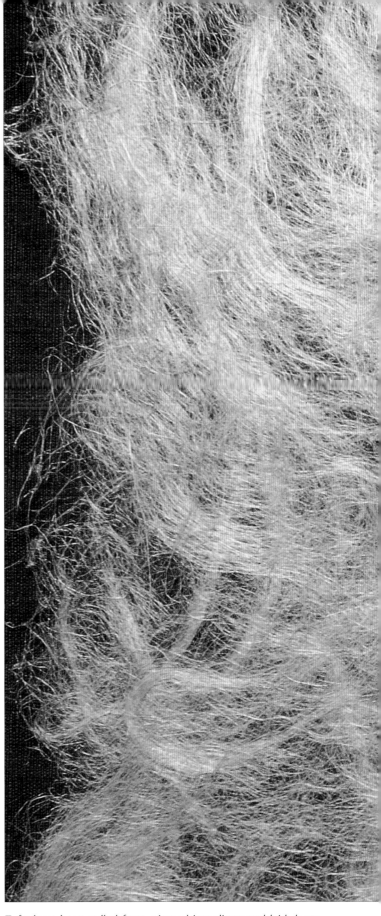

Tufts have been pulled from crimped jute slivers and laid down in overlapping rows as described on page 37. Fibre papers such as this make an ideal base for embroidery, since their neutral tones act as a foil to subsequent embellishment. They can also be dramatically distressed by pulling holes into them or by burning areas of them with a pyrography tool, for example.

INCLUSIONS

It is possible to enhance both the surface texture and the overall design of silk paper by adding inclusions to the fibre during the felting process. The subtle colours of petals, seeds and leaves work very well with undyed fibres, whilst the vibrant colours of threads and ribbons can make stunning inclusions for coloured paper.

You can include fresh **flower petals** from the garden or a special bouquet, perhaps. You can also use dried flowers, either pressed whole or rescued from an elderly consignment of potpourri.

Some **seeds** can be used as inclusions – small flat ones are the most successful. However, by their very nature, seeds are likely to have a high moisture content, which can cause discolouration (foxing) of the finished paper. Unfortunately, there is no way of determining in advance which seeds are likely to be the biggest culprits. **Seed heads** such as honesty, work beautifully.

Fresh leaves make wonderful inclusions and will add a dramatic leafy contrast to stark white silk. You can use the fresh greens of spring through to the golden

colours of autumn. **Dried leaves**, unless carefully preserved, tend to be less successful, as they can disintegrate on felting. However, **skeleton leaves**, handled with a delicate touch, are wonderful.

All kinds of **embroidery threads** and **ribbons** can be included, and their colours will add a sparkling vibrancy to silk paper. Collect the trimmings from a needlework project and sprinkle them over the fibres before felting to add delicate colour and texture to an otherwise plain surface. Alternatively, snip short lengths of exotic embroidery yarns over the fibres.

It is also possible to add wisps of **other fibres** to a sheet of undyed silk paper at the felting stage. These could include glitzy nylons to add a seasonal sparkle, tussah silk tufts to add a cream-on-white marbled quality, or hand-dyed silk fibre fragments to introduce islands of colour.

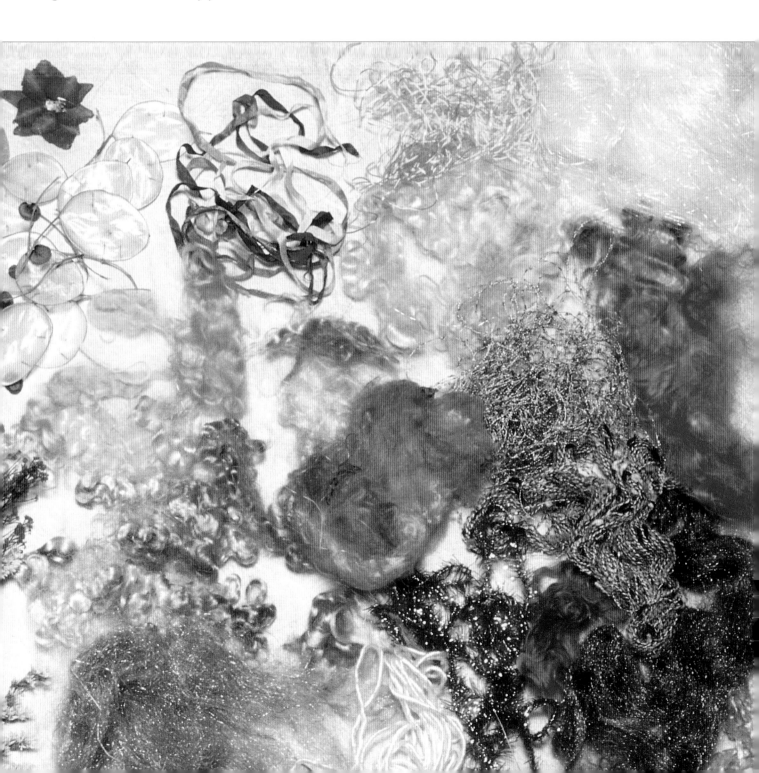

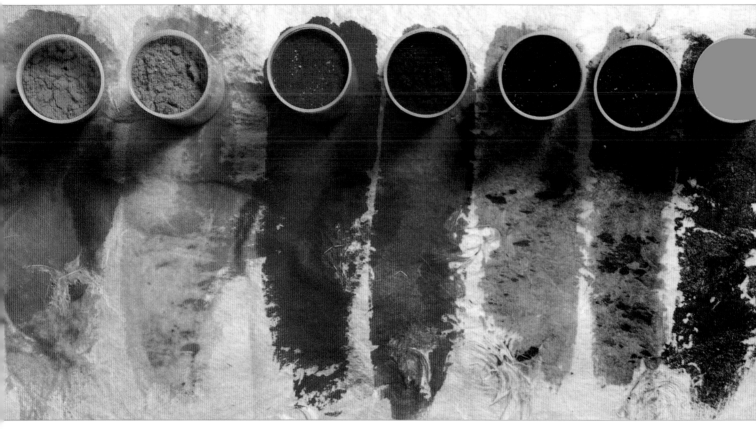

Acid dyes – warm and cool tones of yellow, red and blue and a black are all you need to create any colour you choose.

DYEING EQUIPMENT

As you can see from the photograph opposite, most of the equipment you will need for dyeing silk fibres can be found around the home. However, it goes without saying that all equipment used for dyeing should remain dedicated to that purpose. It is particularly important to keep a close eye on measuring spoons, and to make sure that the saucepans used for dyeing purposes are neither made from aluminium nor subsequently filled with custard!

Silk is made up of layers of protein – its fibres are triangular in cross-section and reflect light like prisms, hence the pearly lustre. Although it is possible to dye silk using cold water, fibre reactive dyes – the kind used for cotton and other cellulose fibres – I prefer to use heat-set, **acid dyes** which usually produce a richer intensity and vibrancy of hue. They are called acid dyes because they use an acid solution to mordant (prepare) the silk fibres for dyeing.

Safety first

Care should be taken when handling and using all dyestuffs; they are best treated as any other potentially harmful domestic substance, such as strong bleaches or garden poisons. Wear a suitable safety mask when measuring out dye powders and gloves when immersing hands into dye solutions. Do not let children handle dyes unless they are supervised, and avoid disposing of spent solutions where pets are likely to be sniffing around.

Make up dye solutions in a **small measuring jug** and measure out the dye powder with a **teaspoon** or measuring spoon. Add a few drops of **washing-up liquid** to the dye powder to assist in creating a smooth dye paste. Mix the dye paste with a **chopstick** or stirring rod. Store the made up dye solutions in leak-proof, **screw-top jars**. They can be stored in this way for several weeks.

Use a small plastic **washing-up bowl** as a mordant bath in which to prepare the fibres for dyeing. Make up a mordant solution of water and **white vinegar**. The vinegar provides the necessary acid content of the mordant solution.

A **microwave-proof dish** can be used as a dye-bath. You can use **pouring jugs**, **syringes**, **turkey basters** and **pipettes** to apply the diluted dyestuff to the prepared fibres. An **artist's** or **wallpaper roller** can be used to help the dye penetrate into any dense areas of fibre.

Acid dyes must be heat fixed. I use a **microwave oven** to fix the dyes but you can also use a **steamer** or a **saucepan** and **colander**. Microwave ovens are unlikely to be used exclusively for dyeing, so they must be stringently protected. I enclose the dye-soaked fibres in **cellulose kitchen wrap** prior to fixing the dye in a microwave oven.

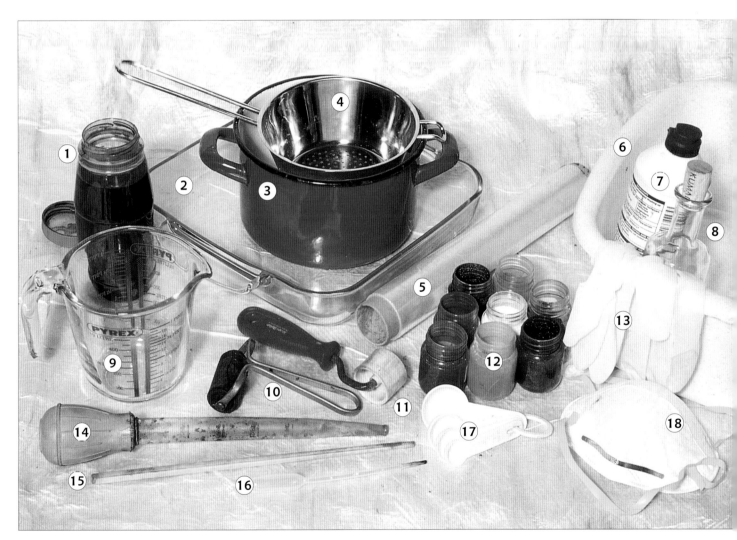

The tool and materials required for dyeing silk fibres.

1. Screw-top jars
2. Microwave-proof dish
3. Saucepan
4. Colander
5. Cellulose kitchen wrap
6. Washing-up bowl
7. Washing-up liquid
8. White vinegar
9. Measuring jug
10. Artist's roller
11. Wallpaper roller
12. Acid dye powders
13. Protective gloves
14. Turkey baster
15. Chopstick/stirring rod
16. Pipette
17. Measuring spoons
18. Face mask

PAPERMAKING EQUIPMENT

The photograph opposite includes both essential and optional equipment needed to make paper from silk. Everything can usually be found around the home, and can be washed and replaced in the drawer or cupboard after use.

Cellulose paste powder is mixed with water and used to 'felt' the silk fibres. Normal wallpaper paste is ideal for beginners, but for serious textile projects it is better to use an archival quality, pure methyl cellulose paste which is available from specialist papermaking suppliers. This does not contain additives or fungicides that could rot the silk fibres. You will also need a **small mixing bowl** in which to prepare the paste, a **teaspoon** to measure out the paste powder and a **chopstick** or **stirring rod** to mix the powder with water.

Opened out **newspapers** protect the work surface and absorb excess paste.

A **plastic sheet** is used as a barrier between the felting net and protective newspapers. It should be slightly larger than the net. Use a heavyweight plastic (cut from a heavy duty carrier bag) as a flimsy plastic sheet may ruckle up during the felting process.

Net is used to support the silk fibres during the felting process. You will need a minimum of two pieces, each at least 5cm (2in) bigger all round than the proposed sheet of paper. Although you can use any type of net, best results will be achieved with a heavy-duty type that can be found at builders' merchants, papermaking suppliers or, possibly, some garden centres.

Those of you who have skin allergies, or lesions, who still want a hands-on experience should protect them with a **barrier cream**.

Small, sharp **scissors** are useful for cutting silk fibres to length and for preparing some types of inclusions.

I like to felt the fibres with my hands. However, if you do not want to get sticky fingers, use a piece of **sponge** to apply the paste to the fibres.

A **spray bottle** filled with clean water can be used to dampen thick beds of fibre prior to felting, and to dampen dry sheets of paper prior to moulding.

The felted paper can be left to dry flat on the work surface or hung on a washing line with **clothes pegs**.

A **flat-bladed knife** or thin spatula is used to release dried paper from the felting net and moulds.

You can create three-dimensional objects by moulding silk paper over **wooden, ceramic, glass and plastic moulds.** You can even mould over your hand! However, do consider the shape of the mould, and make sure that you will be able to get the moulded paper off in one piece!

Cover glass or plastic moulds with **cellulose food wrap** to help release dry moulded paper. It is also used when fixing dyes (see page 30). On wooden moulds, apply a thin layer of **vegetable oil** to protect the wood and help release the moulded paper.

A **nail board** is an optional extra for use when working with mawata caps. It should be made from a thick sheet of plywood or medium-density fibreboard (MDF). You will also need some **wire nails**, preferably with the heads removed, and a **hammer.**

Opposite
The tools and materials
required to make silk paper.
  1. Wooden mould
  2. Water spray bottle
  3. Ceramic moulds
  4. Chopstick/stirring rod
  5. Small mixing bowl
  6. Vegetable oil
  7. Sponge
  8. Teaspoon
  9. Cellulose paste powder
  10. Cellulose food wrap
  11. Barrier cream
  12. Flat-bladed knife
  13. Net
  14. Plastic sheet
  15. Newspaper
  16. Scissors
  17. Clothes pegs
  18. Nail board, hammer
      and wire nails

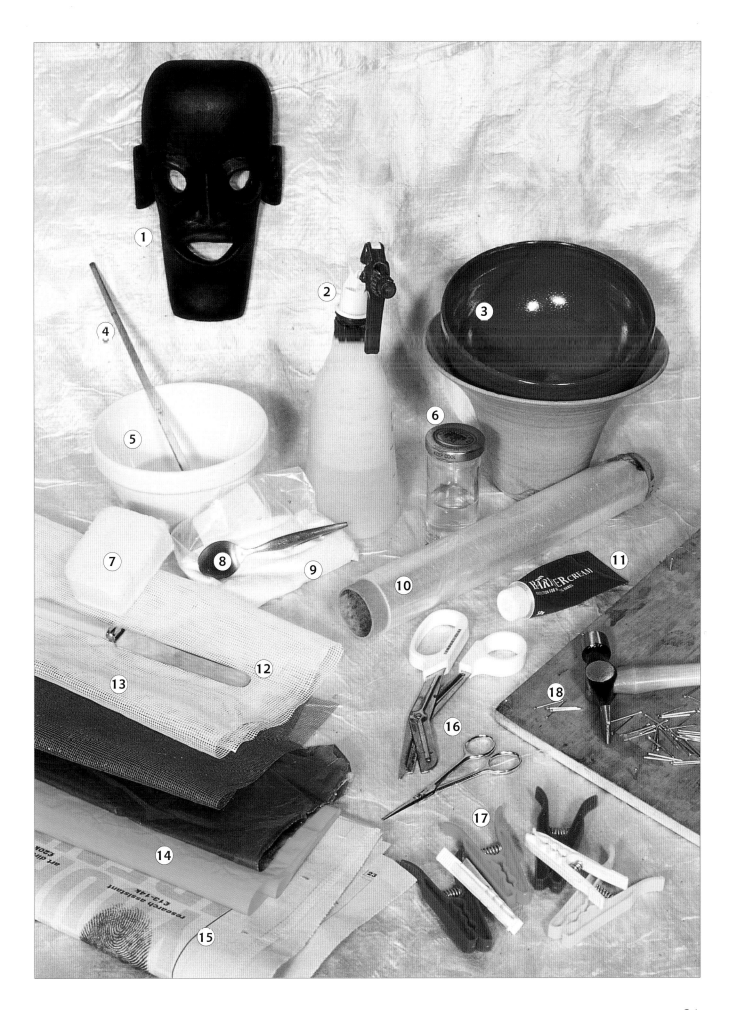

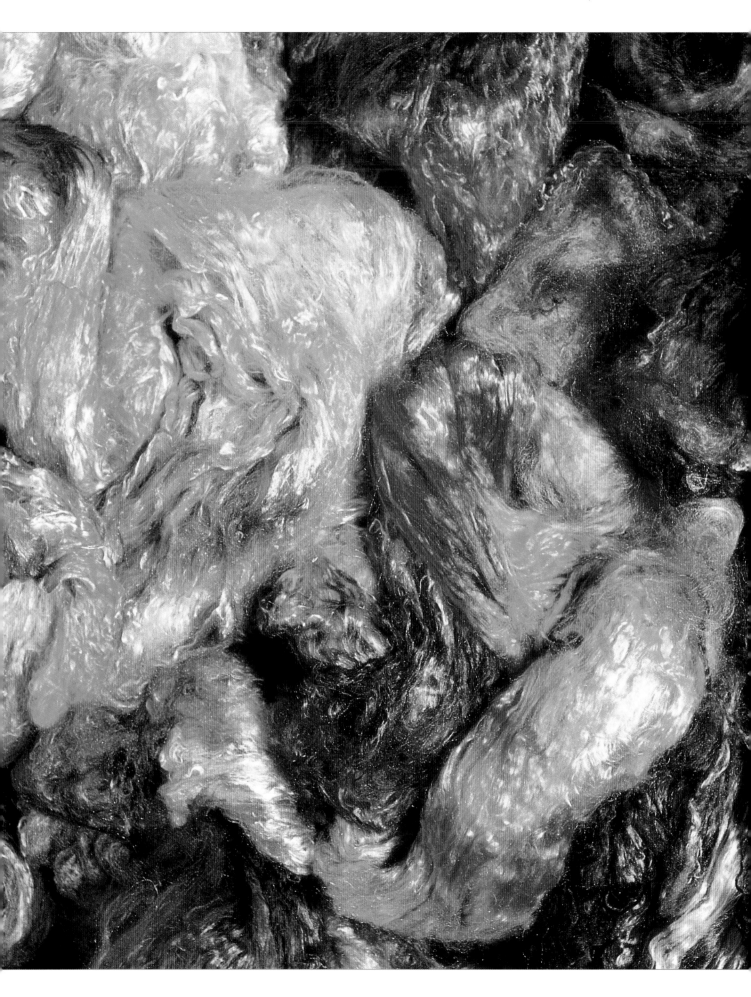

Dyeing silk fibres

An infinite variety of papers can be made using coloured fibres as a starting point. You can buy hand-dyed fibres as well as factory-dyed ones, but it is very easy – and much more satisfying – to dye your own. Silk is a protein substance and, although it is possible to colour silk fibres with cold water, fibre reactive dyes, much more vibrant results are achieved using heat-set acid dyes. This chapter explodes the myth that acid dyeing is either difficult or dangerous. The only acid used is white vinegar.

The step-by-step instructions show you how to mordant the fibres, how to make up and store stock solutions, how to apply the dyestuff to the fibres and finally how to fix the dye colours. I use a microwave oven to fix the dye colours, so the following instructions show how the fibres are prepared for this method. However, I also show alternative methods of fixing dyes.

Hand-dyed silk tops.

MORDANTING FIBRES

Before applying heat-set, acid dyes, the silk fibres must be prepared (mordanted) in a weak acid solution of water and white vinegar. A few drops of washing-up liquid will assist the wetting of the fibres. The solution is completely harmless and you do not have to wear protective gloves when immersing the fibres in the mordant bath.

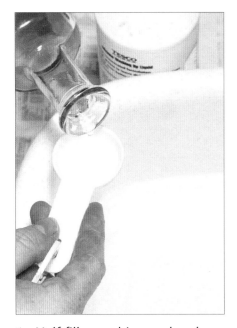

1. Half fill a washing-up bowl with warm water, add two or three drops of washing-up liquid and then four tablespoons of white vinegar. Stir the solution well to disperse the vinegar.

2. Immerse all the fibres to be dyed in the mordant bath and leave them to thoroughly wet out for at least two hours. If more convenient, fibres can be left to mordant overnight. However, they will begin to smell if left in the mordant bath for longer periods.

PREPARING THE DYE SOLUTION

The following instructions show you how to make a 1% stock solution of dye. This will produce a medium shade of colour. If you need a strong, deep shade, double the quantity of dye powder. For paler shades dilute the stock solution with half as much water again. Stock solutions will keep for several weeks if stored in screw-top jars. Be very careful to label each jar before storage. Make up stock solutions of each dye colour you intend to use. For beginners, I suggest making up just seven stock solutions – warm and cool shades of red, yellow and blue and a black. These can be mixed to produce all the colours you need.

Dye powders are very fine, so I would advise that you wear a face mask when handling them.

1. Put two level teaspoons of dye powder in a measuring jug. Wear a pair of protective gloves if you want to keep your hands clean.

2. Add two or three drops of washing-up liquid.

3. Now add just enough warm water to form a paste and stir until smooth.

4. Slowly add boiling water to the paste until you have 500ml (1pint) of solution. Stir the mixture continuously until the dye powder has fully dissolved.

5. Leave to cool then pour the stock solution into screw-top jars. Label and store until required.

DYEING THE FIBRES

Dye colour can be applied to silk fibres in different ways, but I prefer the method known as space dyeing. Stock dye solutions are selectively placed on the 'spaces' of the fibre mass using various types of applicator. The results can be quite startling – from a random variegated distribution of colour to a beautifully controlled rainbow.

You can also apply dry dye powder to the fibres and then pour boiled water on to them. This method also results in random colour distribution but with lots of subtle shades (see page 28).

If you want a solid colour, you can boil the fibres in a saucepan of dye solution (see page 29).

Space dyeing

1. Line a microwave-proof dish with a long length of cellulose kitchen wrap. Lay another long length across the dish, at right angles to the first one.

2. Gently squeeze excess mordant solution from the wetted fibres and place them in the dish.

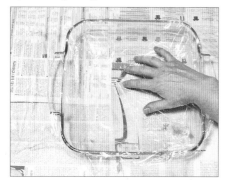

3. Cover large areas of fibre with dye poured from a jug, squirted from a squeezy bottle . . .

4. . . . or from a turkey baster. A baster will often cover bigger spaces more quickly.

5. When the bulk of fibre mass is covered, use a pipette to fill small, defined areas of colour.

6. When all the fibres appear to be covered with colour, squeeze them with a gloved hand to encourage the dye to penetrate into the fibres . . .

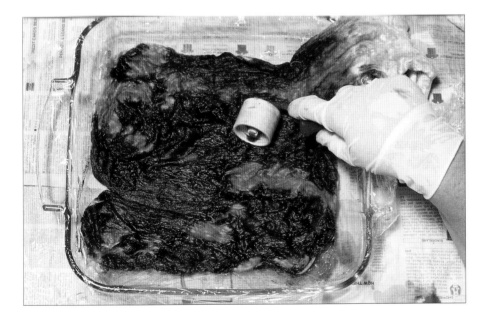

7. . . . or use a small roller to press the dye into the fibres.

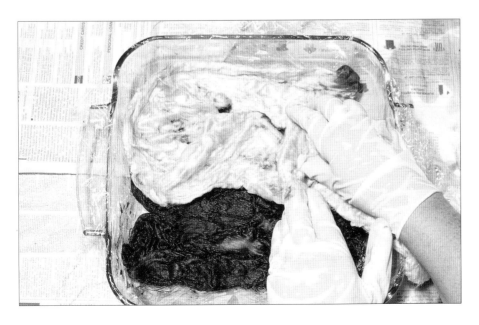

8. When you are sure that dye has penetrated this first layer of fibres, spread a second layer on top and colour this as steps 3–7. If you plan to fix the dyes in a microwave oven, it is best not to attempt more than three layers at a time. Fix the dye colours as shown on page 30.

Dry dyeing

Throwster's waste and hanked filaments take up dye colour quickly and easily. Although there is no reason why they cannot be dyed using the space dyeing method, you might equally choose to use the dry dyeing process shown below. This method is particularly useful if you need to produce different textures in related colourways. I have used just two layers, but you could stack several layers of different kinds of fibres each on its own sheet of net. Each successive layer will receive a slightly diluted dye strength, and the papers made from them will therefore reflect differing intensities of the same colour range.

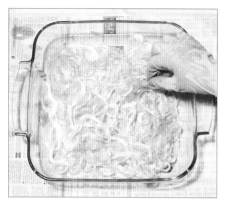

1. Arrange a bed of mordanted throwster's waste in the bottom of a microwave-proof dish.

2. Use clothes pegs to secure a sheet of net stretched across the top of the dish.

3. Cut two lengths of hanked filament, spread out the fibres and lay them on top of the net.

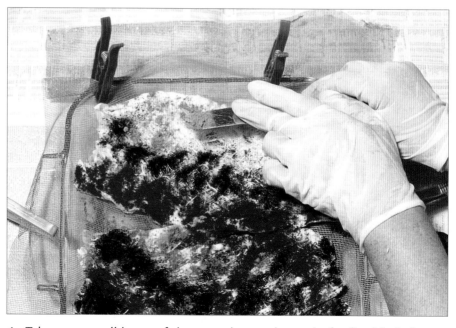

4. Take up a small heap of dye powder on the end of a flat-bladed knife and gently tap the knife to distribute the powder over the filament. Repeat with other colours.

5. Carefully pour small quantities of boiled water over the dye powders. The dye will dissolve and spread into the silk filament. Excess coloured water will pass through the filament on to the throwster's waste.

6. Immediately all the dye powder has dissolved remove the dyed silk filaments and the net, and carefully pour away the excess coloured water from the dish of throwster's waste. Wrap the fibres in cellulose kitchen wrap and fix the colours as shown on page 30.

Creating strong, even colours

Sometimes you may want to produce evenly coloured sheets of silk paper. To achieve this, prepare a dye solution in a saucepan. Completely immerse mordanted fibres in the solution and boil for 20 minutes, stirring frequently. Because the fibres are able to move freely during the dyeing process, they absorb the dye evenly producing a very uniform colour. Remove the fibres from the saucepan then rinse and dry them as shown on page 31.

FIXING THE DYES

Acid dyes must be steam fixed and, having placed the dye carefully on the fibres, the colours must be fixed *in situ* if they are to remain distinct. I wrap the dyed fibres in cellulose kitchen wrap and fix the dye colours in a microwave oven. The kitchen wrap creates a steam chamber, which helps reduce the fixing time and also stops the oven getting dirty.

However, if you do not have a microwave (or would prefer not to use one) there are alternatives. If you have a steamer that can be dedicated to non-food use, then do use that. You can also fix colours by putting the fibres in a colander placed over a saucepan of boiling water.

Steam fixing in a microwave oven

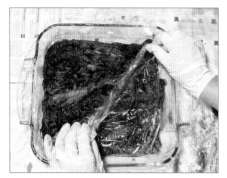

1. When you have dyed all the fibres, fold in the ends of one length of cellulose kitchen wrap then fold in those at right angles to form a completely sealed package.

2. Place the dish in a microwave and 'cook' for five to seven minutes on full power. Place the dish on a sheet of plastic to guard against accidental leakage.

3. Remove the dish and check both sides of the package for white patches. Small areas of white on the surface could indicate large areas of undyed fibre in the middle of the bundle.

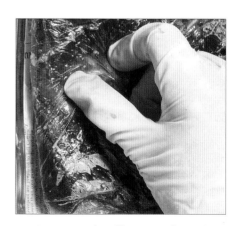

4. Squeeze the fibres to disperse dye colour into the white areas. Microwave the package again for three to four minutes, longer if the bundle of fibres is quite thick or if a turquoise dye has been used.

5. Allow the package to cool, then remove the kitchen wrap and immerse the fibres in a bowl of warm soapy water. Swish the fibres because the soap also acts as a setting agent. Rinse the fibres in several changes of water, until the water runs clear, then hang them up outside or leave them to dry in an airing cupboard. You can dry some fibres (but not silk tops) in a tumble drier.

Other methods of steam fixing

Place the dyed fibres in a steamer or in a stainless steel colander placed over a saucepan of boiling water. Steam for 15–20 minutes. If you are impatient, you can reduce the 'cooking' time by 5 minutes by covering the colander with a lid. Carefully turn the fibres once or twice to distribute the heat evenly.

Alternatively, put the dyed fibres in a flat, oven-proof dish, cover the dish, place it in a roasting tray half filled with water, and bake in moderate oven for 20–30 minutes, depending on the depth and type of fibre.

Silk fibres dyed with heat-set, acid dyes attain a vibrancy and intensity of colour unsurpassed, in my view, by any other means of dyeing. In particular, throwster's waste (above and right) attains deep saturation levels very easily. By bunching and layering the fibres during the dyeing process, it is also possible to achieve an infinite variety of tone and intensity, often within the same dye batch. Mulberry silk tops (opposite) still retain a high level of lustre provided they are handled with care during the rinsing stage of the dyeing process. It is important not to over-squeeze the wet fibres after rinsing. Your reward will be a glowing mass of jewel-like colours.

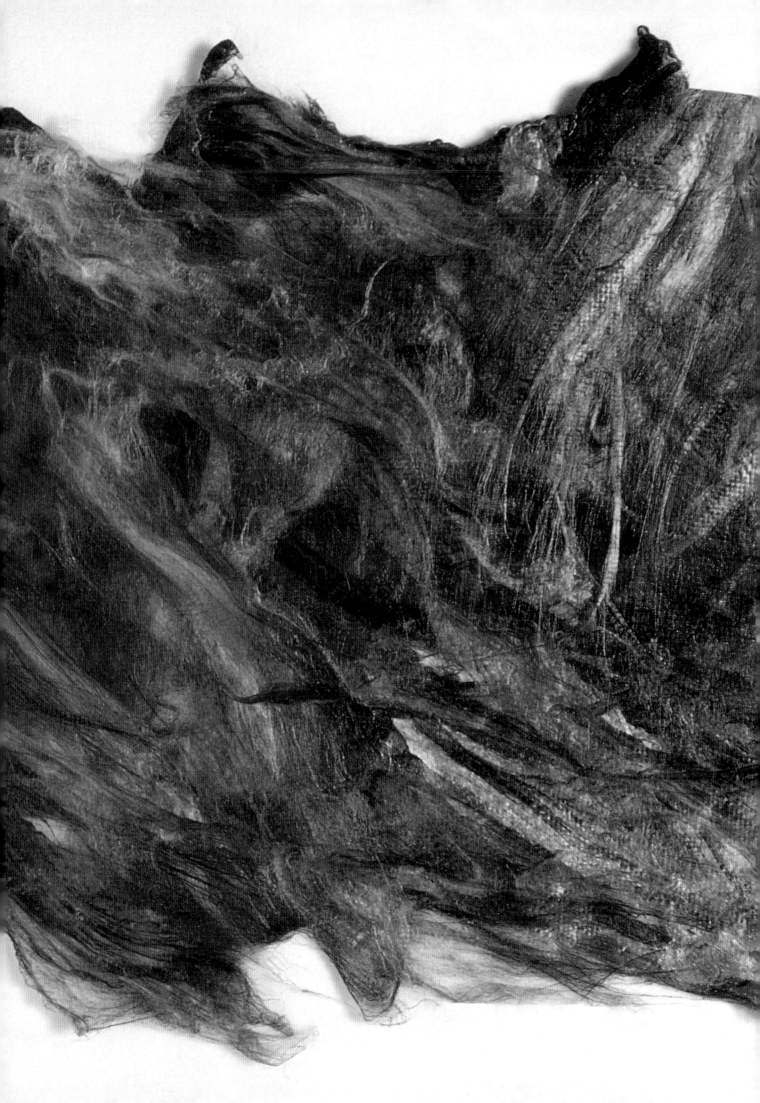

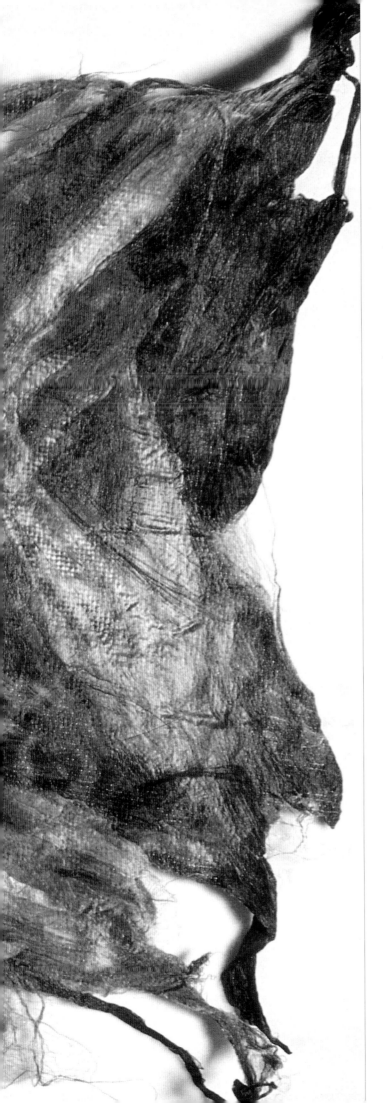

Papermaking – basic techniques

By the time you have worked through this chapter you will have learnt the basic techniques for making paper from silk fibres. There is no substitute for rolling up your sleeves and letting the paste glisten through your fingers.

I take you, step by step, through the basic stages of making a sheet of paper using tufts pulled from undyed silk tops. You will need approximately 25g (1oz) of silk to make a 20 x 30cm (8 x 12in) sheet of paper. You will also need a sheet of plastic and two sheets of net.

Two-tone silk tops paper. I started this paper with a base layer of tufts pulled from black, hand-dyed silk tops and laid on the felting net as shown on pages 36–37. I then added a second layer of blue, hand-dyed silk tops, generally as shown on page 46 but, instead of rotating the fibre bed by 90°, I overlaid these tufts in two asymmetrical rows at 45° to suggest an anarchic mystery. The edges of the paper are deliberately made uneven, for the same reason.

GETTING READY

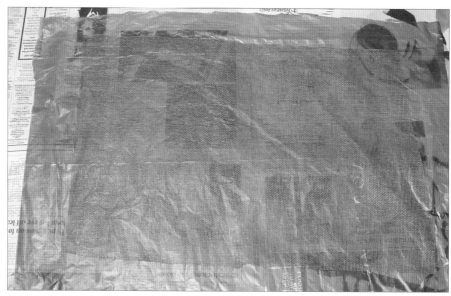

1. Mix up a batch of wallpaper paste. Measure 500ml (1 pint) of cold water into a basin and sprinkle two heaped teaspoons of paste powder on top. Thoroughly stir the mixture and then leave it to stand until thickened (at least half an hour).

2. Cover the work surface with old newspaper. Place a sheet of plastic on the newspaper and then place one of the sheets of net on the plastic.

PREPARING A FIBRE BED

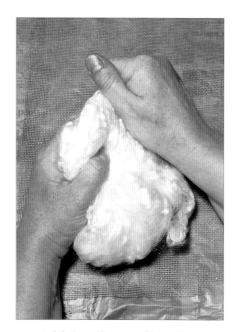

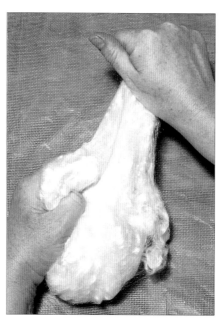

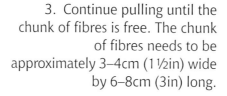

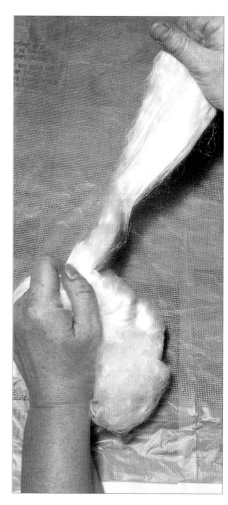

1. Hold the silk tops fibre firmly in the heel of one hand and grip the outer edge with the other hand.

2. Start to pull the fibres apart.

3. Continue pulling until the chunk of fibres is free. The chunk of fibres needs to be approximately 3–4cm (1½in) wide by 6–8cm (3in) long.

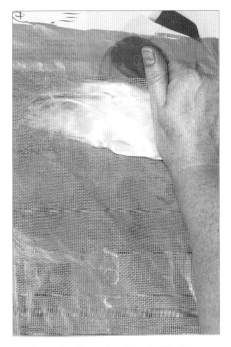

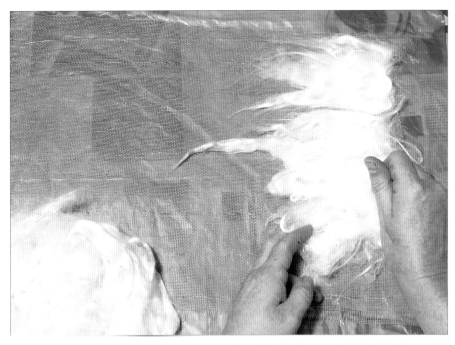

4. Lay the first 'pull' of silk fibres on the net, at the top right-hand corner.

5. Pull more lengths of fibre and overlap them down the side of the net to make a column approximately 20cm (8in) long.

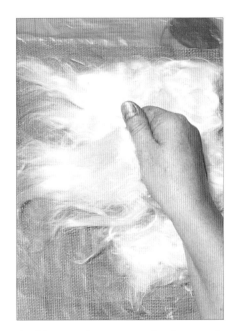

6. Now make a second column of fibres that overlap each other and those in the first column.

7. Continue making more columns of overlapping fibres until an area, say, 20 x 30cm (8 x 12in) of the net is covered.

FELTING THE FIBRES

This is the stage where the fun starts, and you work the paste into the fibres. If you are not happy applying glue by hand, wear rubber gloves or use a piece of sponge.

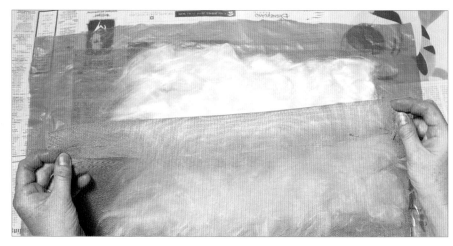

1. Carefully cover the prepared fibres with the other sheet of net.

2. Scoop up a handful of paste from the bowl and place it on the centre of the net. Work with a firm circular movement to press the paste through the net and into the silk fibres.

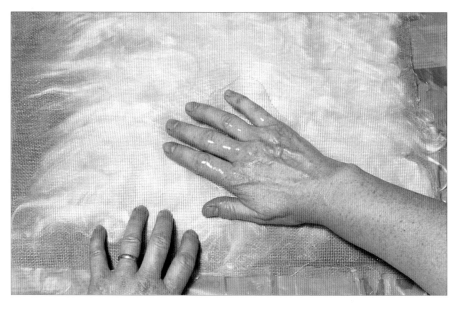

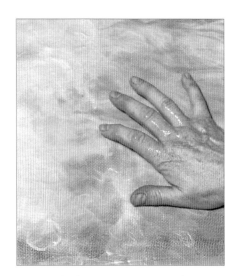

3. Work the paste into the fibres until they are thoroughly wetted.

4. Turn the whole 'sandwich' of nets and fibre over and check for missing links (dry areas).

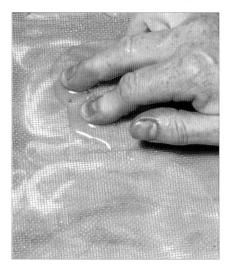

5. Apply more paste to these areas (and, for good measure, to the rest of the underside) and work this into the fibres.

38

DRYING THE PAPER

The method used to dry the felted fibres will affect the texture of the finished sheet of paper. With the method shown here, the fibres are left to dry while still attached to one sheet of net. The finished sheet of paper will have a textured finish on both sides. On page 48 I show you how to achieve a very smooth surface on one side of the paper.

1. Carefully peel back a corner of the top net from the felted fibre. Release any fibres that start to lift off with the net and carefully press them back into place.

2. Leave the fibres to dry, either flat on the work surface or hang them on a washing line, using clothes pegs to secure the edge of the net, not the fibres, to the line.

3. When the paper is thoroughly dry lay it face down on a flat dry surface and carefully ease up one corner of the net with a craft knife. As the width of free net gets larger, hold the paper flat on the surface with the palm of your hand. Never try pulling the paper off the net. The finished sheet of paper is shown below.

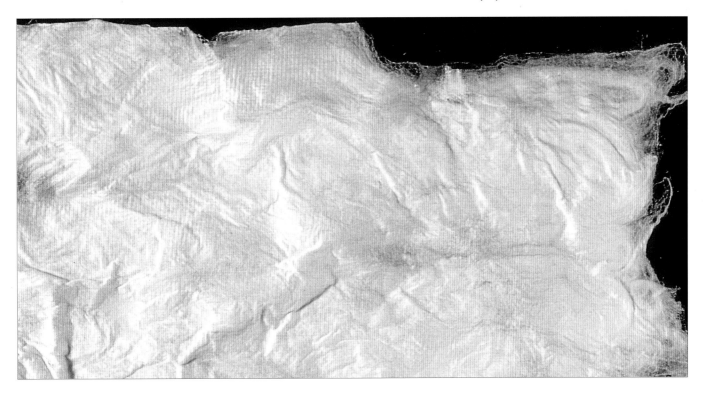

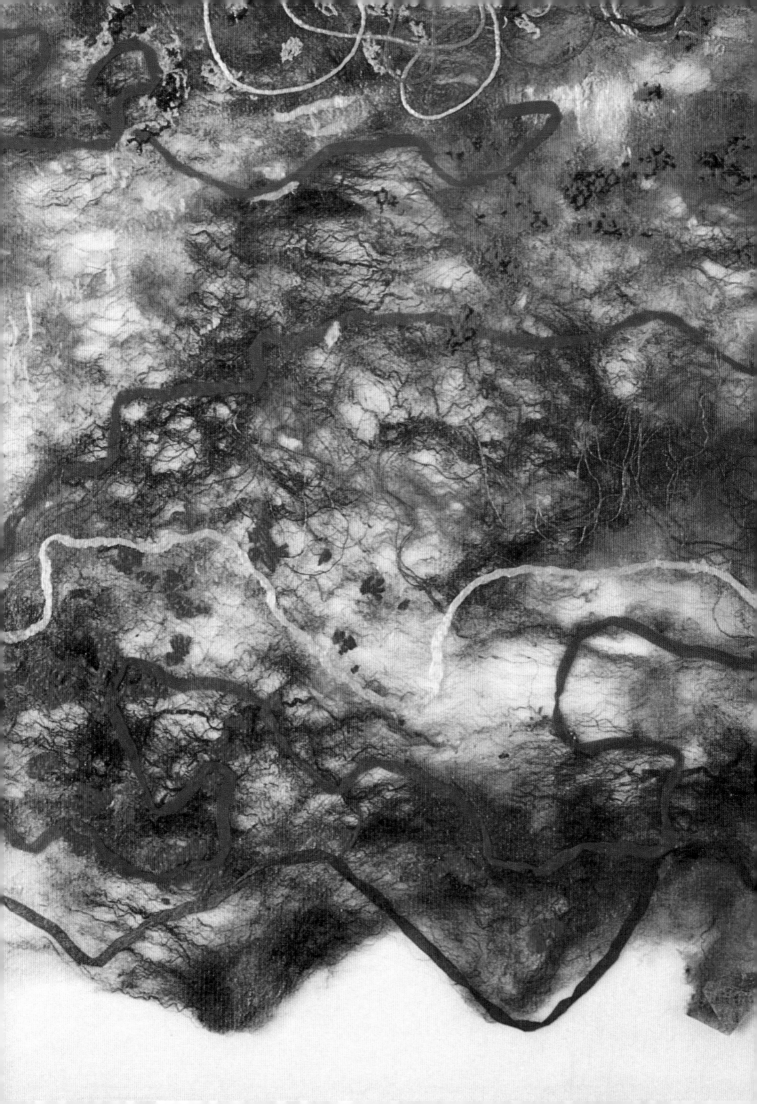

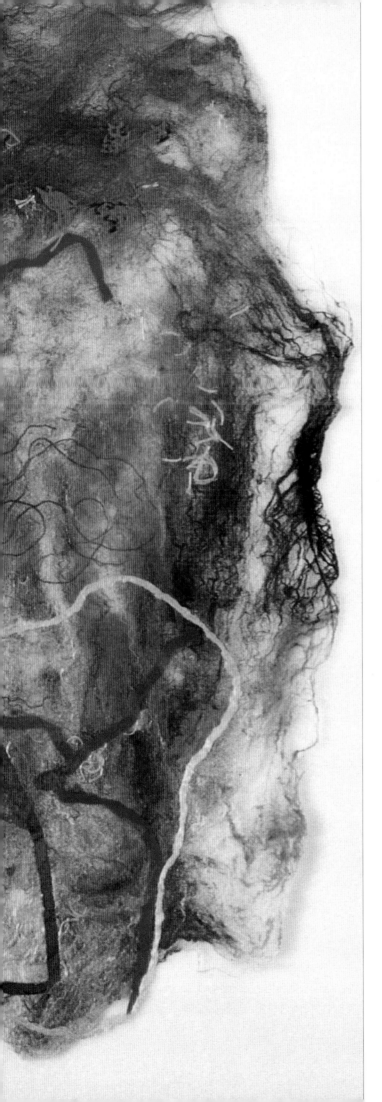

Papermaking – other techniques

In this chapter I show you how to make lots of other types of paper. First, still using silk tops, I show you some variations of the basic technique – changing the arrangement of fibres, combining mulberry and tussah silks, and using inclusions to add subtle colour and texture to undyed fibres.

I then show you how to make completely different sheets of paper using the other types of silk fibre. Silk is immensely strong relative to its mass, and by using these other silks it is possible to produce 'cobweb' papers of robust fragility. In particular, mawata caps and silk handkerchiefs each have a matted centre and a strongly-defined rim which can be used to create stunning designs.

Finally, I have included a few examples of papers made with fibres other than silk.

However, I am sure that, when you get started, you will find lots more ideas of your own to develop.

A thick layer from a hand-dyed mawata cap has been eased flat and then stretched to form the base of this sheet of paper. Silk ribbons, threads and snips of fabric and embroidery floss have been drizzled over the surface and then felted into place. Note how the colours of the embellishments have been chosen to reflect those of the mawata cap base layer.

SILK TOPS VARIATIONS

On this and the following pages I show you how to use silk tops to make other types of paper, simply by making small variations to the basic techniques.

Long-grained paper

For this type of paper the felting bed is made up with long lengths of fibres rather than short tufts as used on pages 36–37.

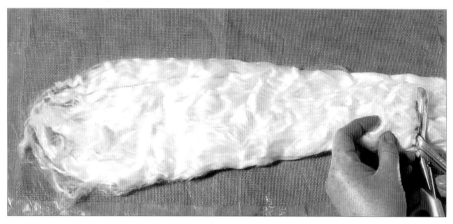

1. Cut a 30cm (12in) length of silk top.

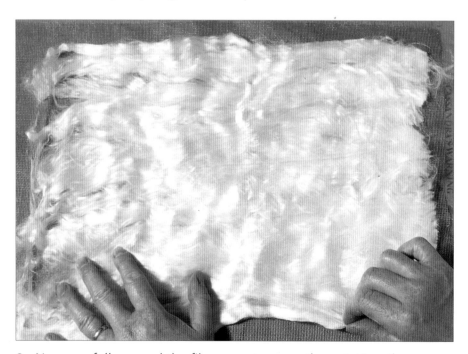

2. Now carefully spread the fibres apart, across the net. Vary the density of fibres to add texture to the finished paper. Cover the fibres with a second net and then finish the paper as shown on pages 38–39.

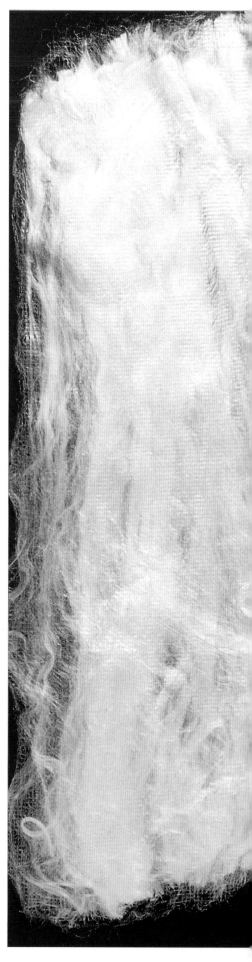

The finished sheet of long-grain, silk tops paper.

Another example of long-grain silk tops paper. For this sheet I used fibres
that were spaced dyed by pouring, rather than by squirting with a baster.

Two-tone silk tops

It is easy to create checks, stripes and random patterns in paper by using different types or colours of silk fibre in the fibre bed prior to felting. Here are two examples of fibre beds and finished papers made using mulberry silk (white fibres) and tussah silk (cream fibres).

This striped effect is created by alternating long lengths of mulberry and tussah silk tops on the fibre bed. The finished paper was felted and then dried using the basic techniques shown on pages 38–39.

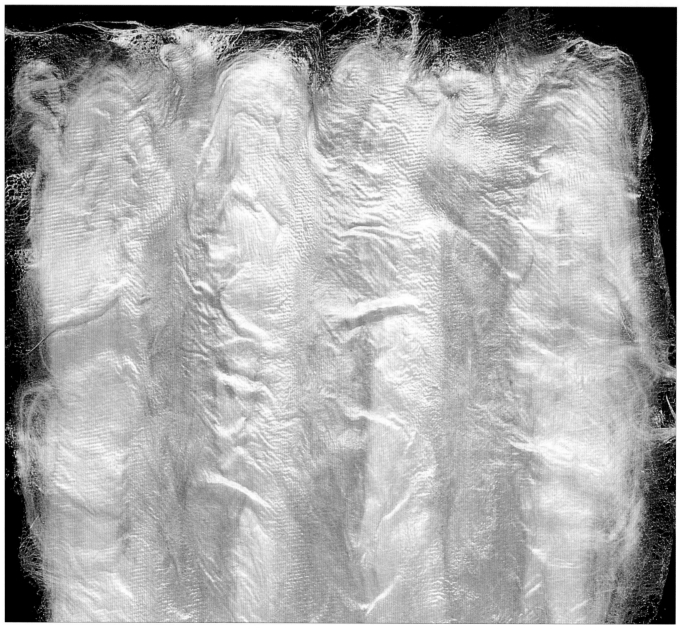

For this check design, alternating squares of different types of silk fibres are overlapped in a similar way to the tufts used on page 37. Each pull of fibre is roughly manipulated into shape and positioned on the fibre bed.

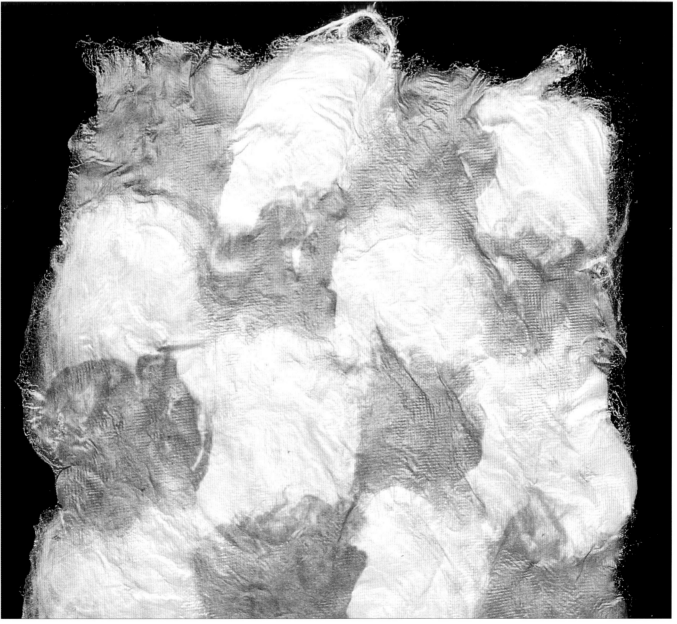

Heavier, double-sided paper

Up until now, the fibre beds have been made using a single layer of silk top fibres. By increasing the number of layers felted a heavier paper can be produced. Also, by using two different types of silk you can create a paper with different colours on either side. In this example I use tufts of mulberry silk tops (white fibres) to make a basic fibre bed as shown on pages 36–37, and then overlaid it with a layer of tufts pulled from tussah silk slivers (cream fibres).

Position a bed of mulberry silk as shown on page 37. Turn the net and fibre bed through 90° and then lay a layer of tussah silk tufts, placing the pulls at right-angles to those in the bottom layer.

When working with multi-layers of fibre, you can help the paste penetrate through a thick fibre bed by spraying the fibres with water before the top net is positioned.

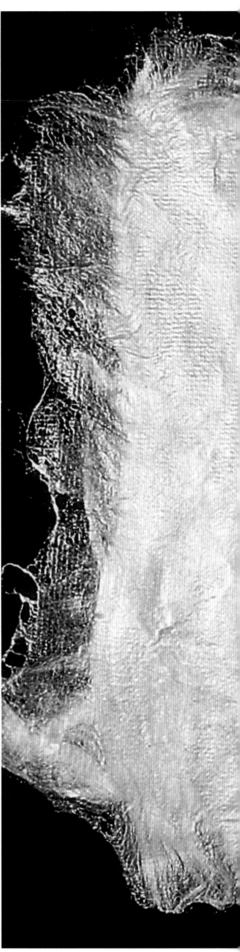

The finished sheet of paper with the tussah silk side uppermost. The small inset picture (opposite) shows the mulberry silk side of the paper.

Smooth paper

You can create a paper that has a very smooth and shiny surface on one side and a textured one on the other by varying the drying method. In this example tufts of silk tops are felted exactly as shown on pages 36–38. Then the top net is removed and the felted fibres are placed, face down, on a smooth flat surface – a stretched sheet of plastic, a sheet of glass or a kitchen worktop or table. The other net is removed and the fibres left to dry naturally on the flat surface.

Interesting alternative under-surfaces can be achieved by placing the wet fibres on to a heavily patterned net curtain, for example.

1. Felt the fibres, remove the top net and then turn the wet fibres, face down, on to a flat smooth surface.

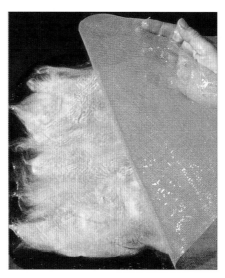

2. Carefully remove the other net.

3. Leave the fibres to dry naturally on the flat surface. Alternatively, you can speed things up by using a hair dryer set on a cool setting.

4. When the paper is completely dry, it will be stuck to the flat surface. If you used a stretched plastic bag, turn paper and plastic over and carefully peel the plastic off the paper. If you used a solid surface, carefully slide a flat blade under the paper and work the paper loose.

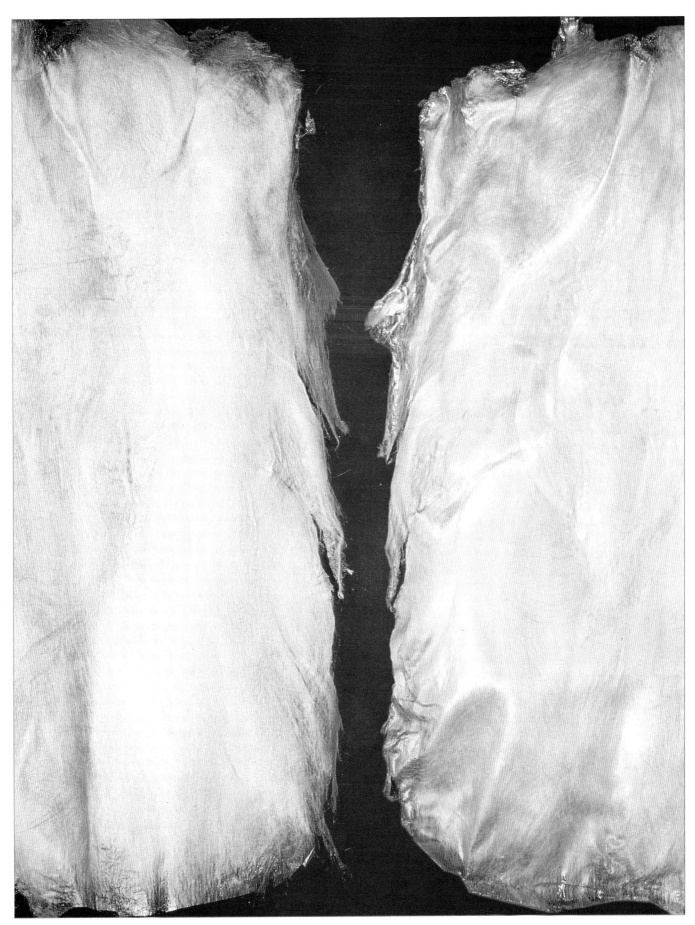

These pictures show both sides of the finished sheet of paper. The top side (left) dried in contact with air, while the smooth shiny underside (right) dried in contact with a smooth surface.

USING INCLUSIONS

It is often interesting, when working with undyed fibres, to add colour and texture by incorporating petals, leaves, threads and glitzy bits. Sprinkle inclusions over the dry fibre bed before felting. In this example a bed of long-grained silk tops is decorated with long lengths of rayon thread and honesty seeds.

1. Make a bed of fibres as shown on page 42 and then place long lengths of rayon (or silk) thread randomly over the surface. Use a fairly thick thread that contrasts with the fine silk fibres.

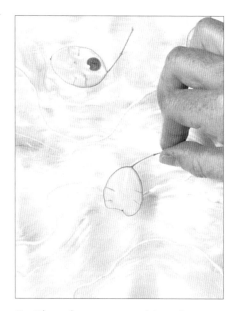

2. Place honesty seed heads randomly over the fibres.

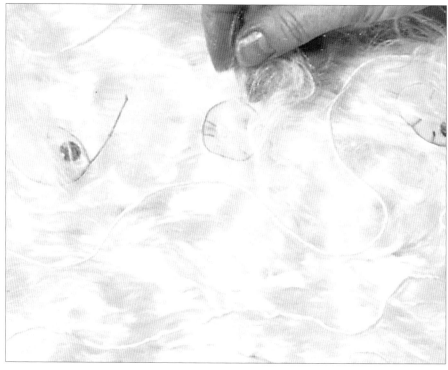

3. Cover larger or non-fibre inclusions with wispy tufts of silk fibre; these will anchor the inclusion but will be virtually invisible on the finished sheet of paper. Finish the paper in the normal way.

Opposite
The finished sheet of paper with rayon thread and honesty seed inclusions. The other sheet is made in a similar manner but with inclusions of fresh garden petals.

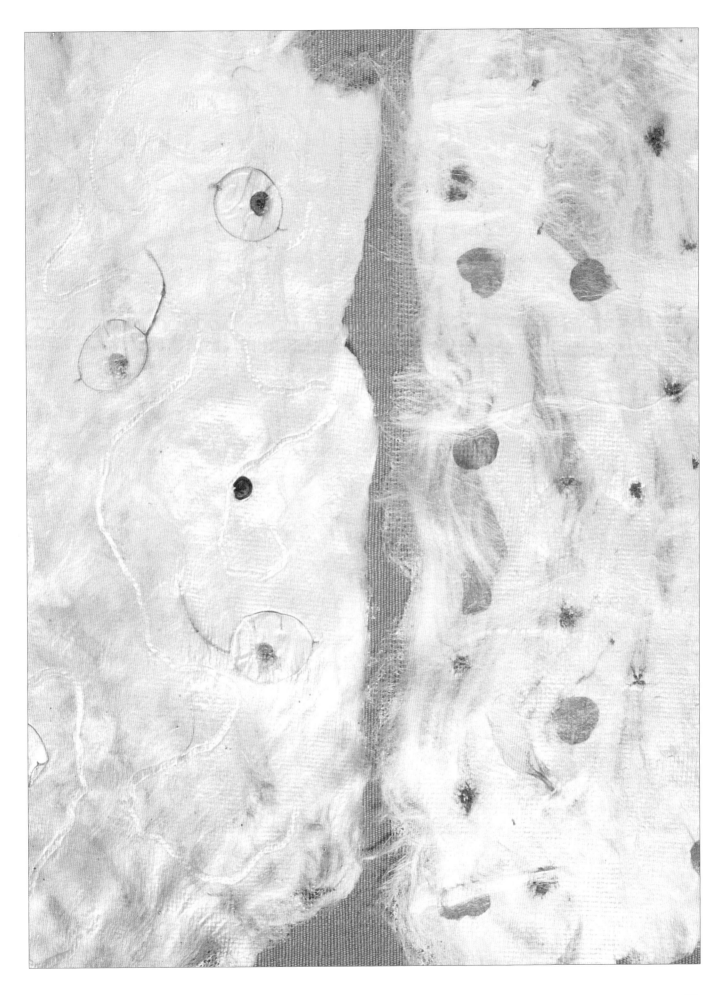

51

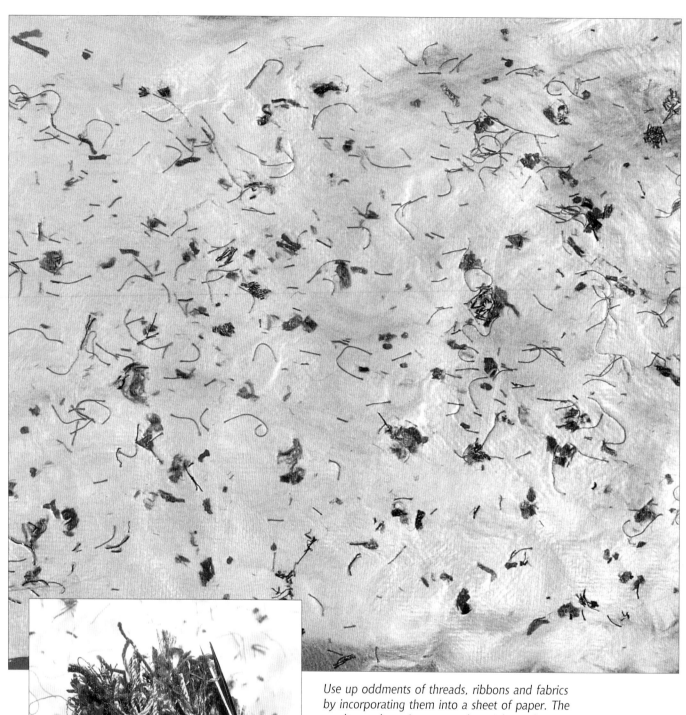

Use up oddments of threads, ribbons and fabrics by incorporating them into a sheet of paper. The results can be quite spectacular as shown here. This sheet of paper is decorated with embroidery thread – I collected together a multicoloured collection of threads and then chopped them into small lengths with a pair of scissors.

Opposite
Beech leaves, fresh from the garden, were placed on top of a long-grain silk tops fibre bed. You can see the wisps of fibres that were used to hold them in place. This is an important precaution when using relatively large pieces of organic matter that would otherwise crinkle and curl as they dry out over several weeks.

USING MAWATA CAPS

Mawata caps are fun to work with. You can exploit the subtle colour variations in the dyeing, and you can make geometric patterns, using the linear quality of the rims to produce unique sheets of cobweb paper. If you can borrow a pair of hands to help stretch out the layers of fibre, all well and good. Otherwise, and sometimes it is more preferable, construct a nailboard to stretch and manipulate the fibres.

1. Prepare a nailboard. You will want a sheet of plywood or MDF, roughly 45 x 30cm (18 x 12in) in size. Gently tap 6–8 small nails along each side, about 1.5cm (½in) in from the edge.

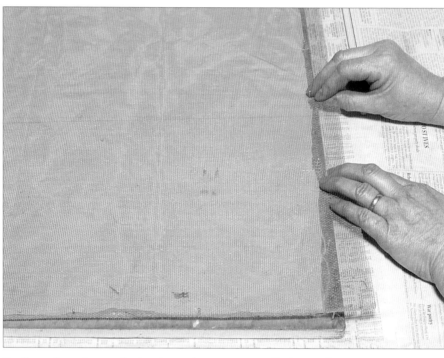

2. Stretch a sheet of plastic and a net over all the nails.

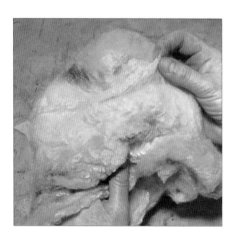

3. Carefully peel off a layer of fibre from the dyed mawata cap.

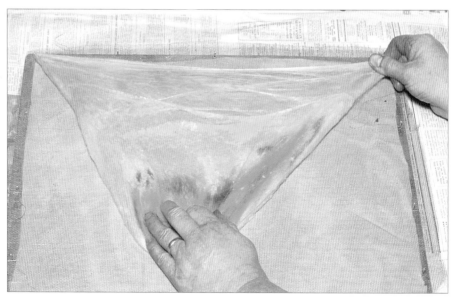

4. Hook the rim of the mawata cap layer over the nail in the left-hand corner of the board and stretch it across to the nail in the right-hand corner. You can be quite forceful when manipulating these fibres.

5. Now pull the cap down the length of the board, to form a long rectangle, and hook it over the nails in the bottom corners of the board.

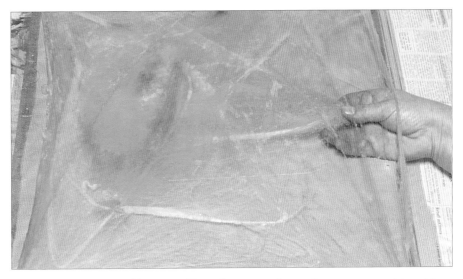

6. Manipulate the fibres, pulling them out from the centre and hooking them over the nails round the edge of the board. Work both the top and bottom layers of the cap.

7. Separate a layer of fibre from a different coloured cap and repeat steps 4–6 on top of the first one. This time, however, work the fibres over a different set of nails. When you are happy with the design, place a second sheet of net over all the nails and felt and finish the paper in the normal way.

Overleaf
The finished sheet of paper should look something like this, but the joy is that, given the infinite possibilities for varying each element of the design, each sheet will be unique.

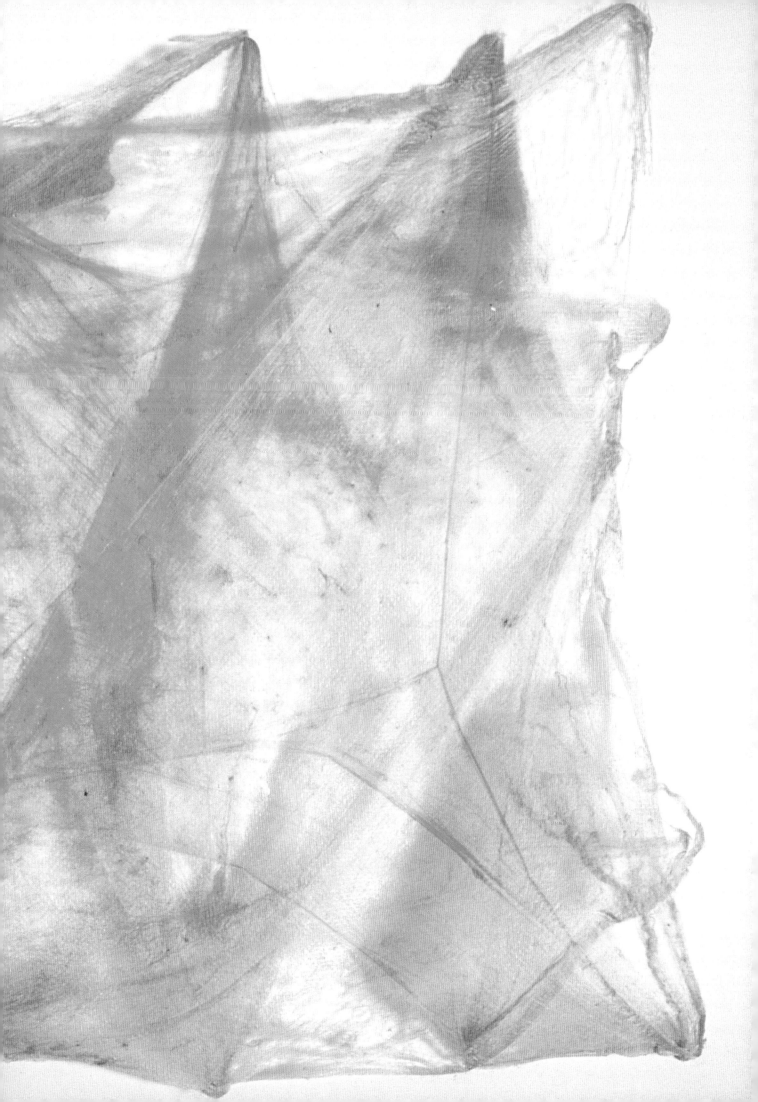

This sheet of paper was made by laminating (gluing) layers of undyed silk handkerchiefs on to a sheet of hand-dyed abaca tissue paper. The tissue was placed on a felting net, but instead of using a nailboard, the handkerchief layers were stretched by hand before being placed on top. When felted, the silken strands adhere to the tissue, creating a filmy, curved linear design and a pearlescent gleam on the surface. Notice how hand-stretching creates much more of an organic design than the geometric patterns produced on a nailboard.

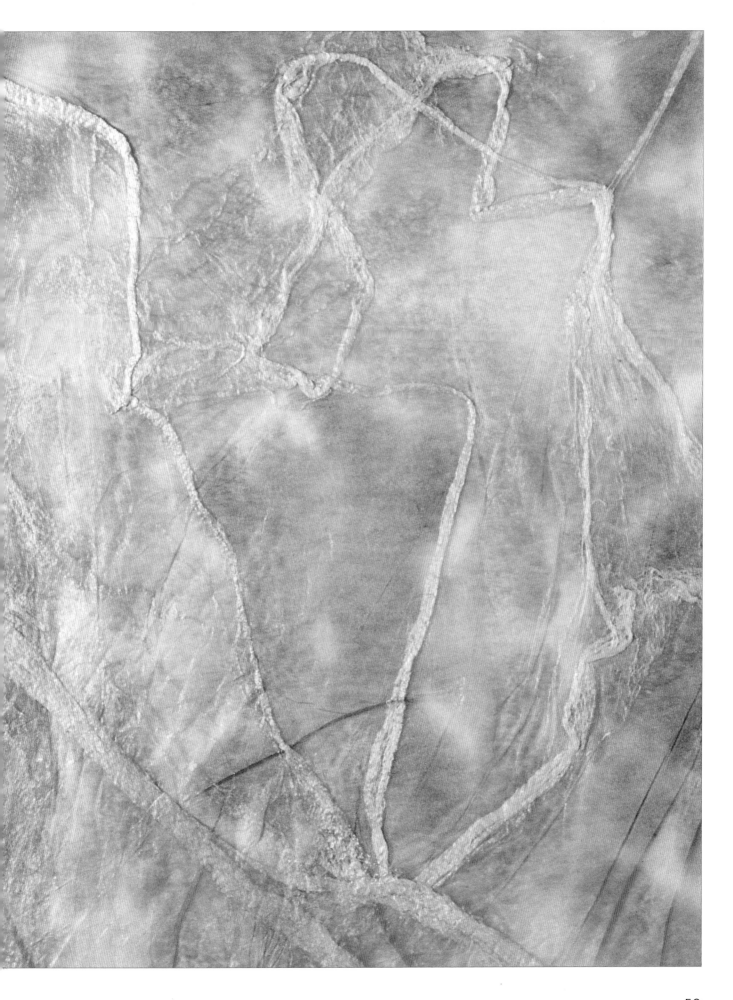

SILK HANDKERCHIEFS AND SILK WADDING

These two types of silk present themselves as a dense mass of fibres, but, with patience, both can be separated into delicately thin layers. If you want to create a base for stitching that requires solid masses of colour, this can easily be achieved by combining layers of each. Similarly, layers of unstretched handkerchiefs can be applied to a fabric base to make a heavier weight of paper (see page 7).

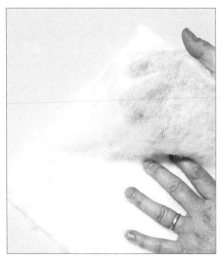

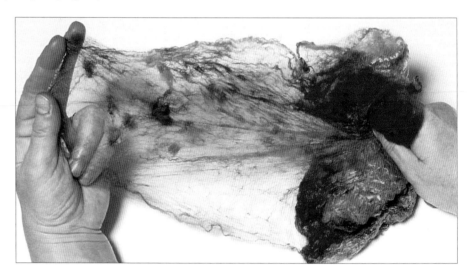

1. Carefully separate a thin layer of undyed silk wadding.

2. Separate single layers of dyed silk handkerchiefs.

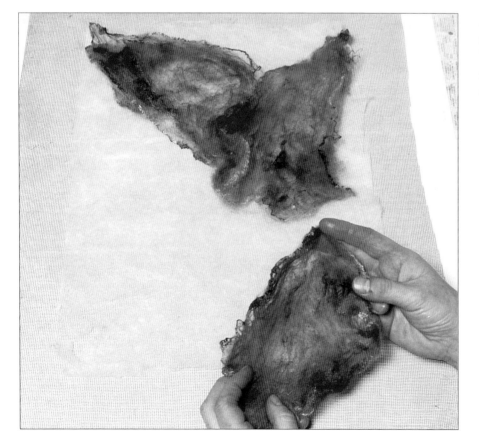

3. Place the silk wadding on a sheet of net and then place the handkerchiefs on top. Cover with a second sheet of net and felt as described on page 38.

Opposite:
The finished paper will be lightweight, colourful, immensely strong and suitable for machine or hand embroidery.

THROWSTER'S WASTE

Throwster's waste consists of relatively short strands of silk fibre. These can be selectively arranged to form a thick bed of entwined tendrils, a delicate gossamer-thin lace or something in between. These fibres are a perfect vehicle for three-dimensional work because they are so easy to customise. When making bowls, arrange the fibres in a circular formation rather than rectangular.

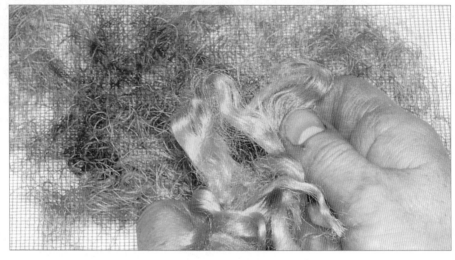

1. Tease out the fibres to create the required consistency.

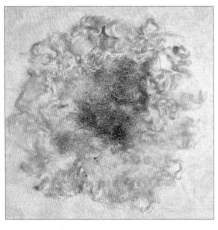

2. Create a circular bed of fibres on a sheet of net and then felt as described on page 38. However, be very careful at the drying stage if your circle is larger than 50cm (20in) in diameter. Large circles must be dried flat and very slowly to avoid buckling.

The finished sheet of paper.

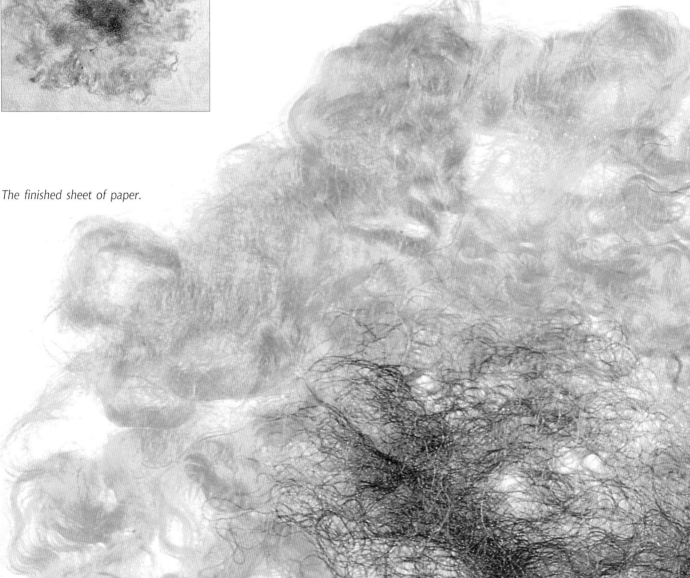

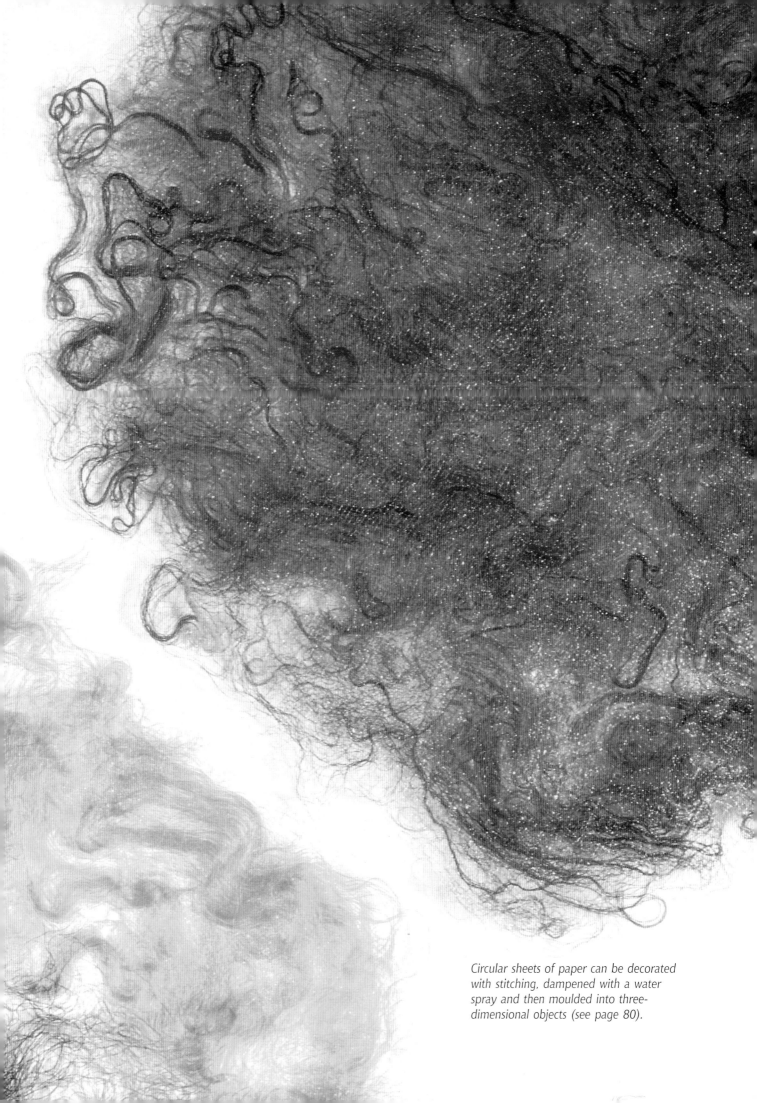

Circular sheets of paper can be decorated with stitching, dampened with a water spray and then moulded into three-dimensional objects (see page 80).

Throwster's waste can be used to make papers with a variety of different textures. In the examples on these pages, interest and movement are created by the variegation in colour and tone of the dyed fibres, as well as the selective placement of lighter and darker tendrils at intervals across the surface. Throwster's waste is usually space dyed, and must be thoroughly dry before felting as it is much easier to handle when bone dry. Although it is perfectly possible to combine dyed fibres from different batches, papers are often more successful if they are made from fibres that have been dyed in the same batch.

HANKED FILAMENTS

It is possible to buy this type of silk in a range of thicknesses (denier) from ultra-fine to coarse and slubby (dupion). All make wonderfully exotic silk papers. When you dye raw silk filaments with heat-set, acid dyes, or if you buy degummed hanks, you will notice that the individual filaments adhere to each other along the length of fibre. When the filaments are teased apart they form a diamond grid which is perfect for papermaking.

Separate a layer of filament and cut it to the required length. Hold the fibres firmly in one hand and gently stretch the fibres with the other until the diamond grid is fully exposed. Lay this 'string vest' of fibres on a sheet of net and felt as shown on page 38. The finished sheet of paper is shown below.

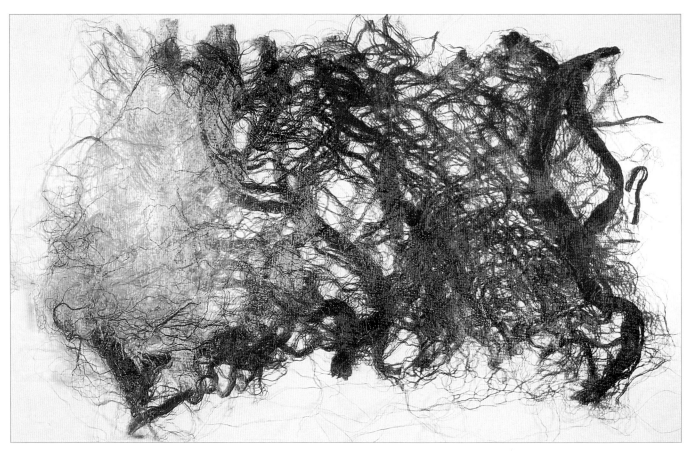

The fibres used to make this paper were dry-dyed as shown on page 28. The intensity of colour is in part due to the direct application of the dye powder. Note that, although only three primary colours (red, blue and yellow) were used, the action of pouring water on them has caused colour blending to produce secondary colours of green and purple.

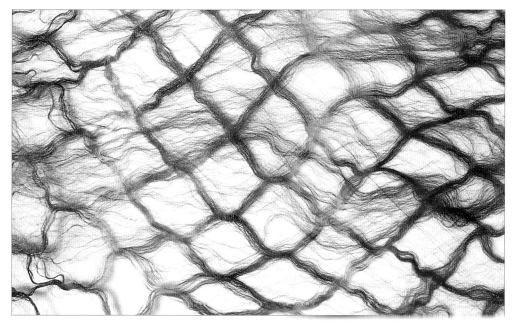

These papers have been made using different types of hanked filaments. Notice how the diamond grid is more regular in the raw silk fibres (those that contain some sericin) than in the commercially degummed fibres. This is a subtle difference but, together with the coarser feel of raw silk, it may influence your choice of fibre for a particular project.

The top paper is made with hand-dyed, raw silk fibres.

The middle sheet is made with heavier weight, degummed, hand-dyed silk which gives a more robust paper.

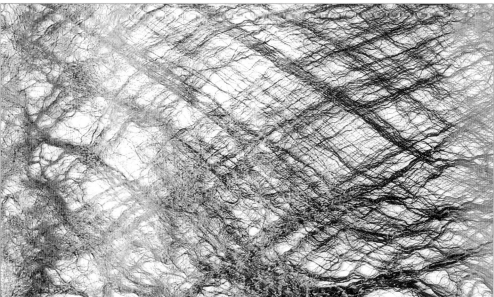

The bottom sheet is made with a fine denier, degummed, hand-dyed silk which produces an altogether more delicate appearance.

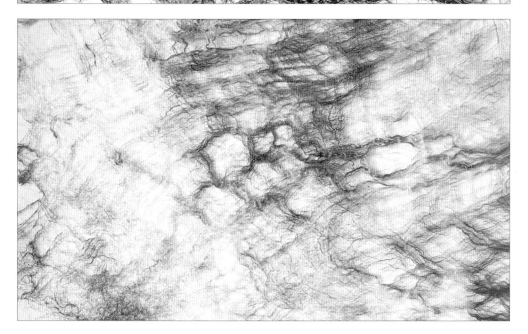

Overleaf
The delicate appearance of this sheet of paper is created by using fine denier, degummed hanked filaments.

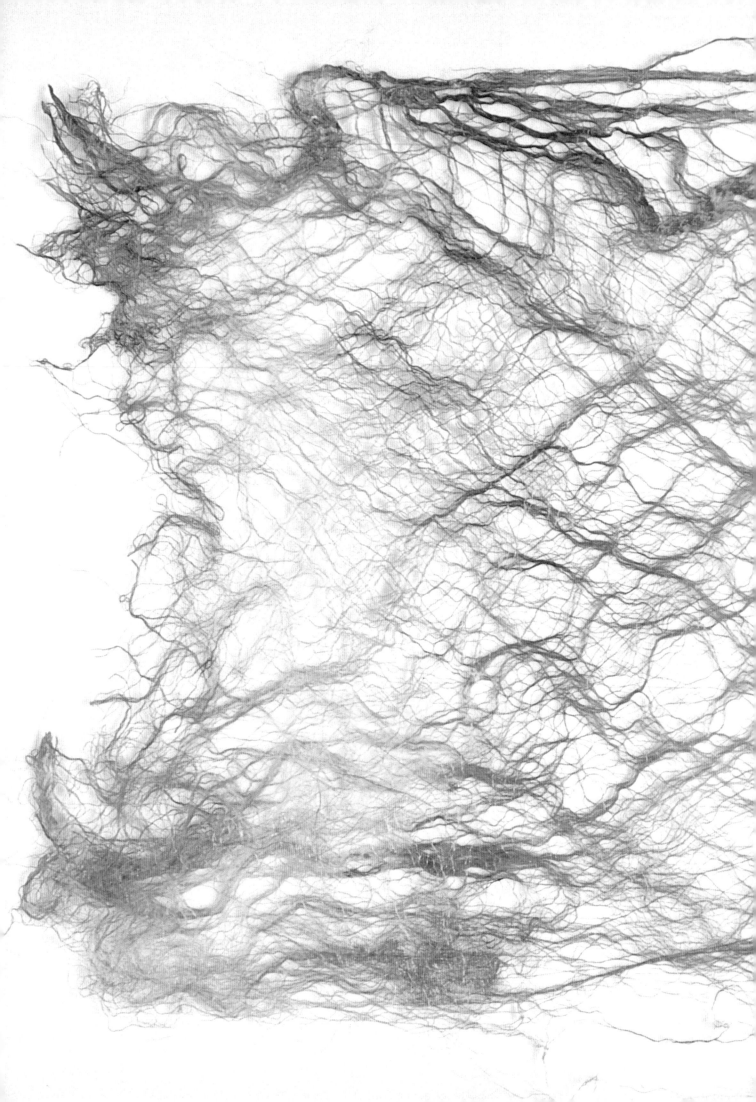

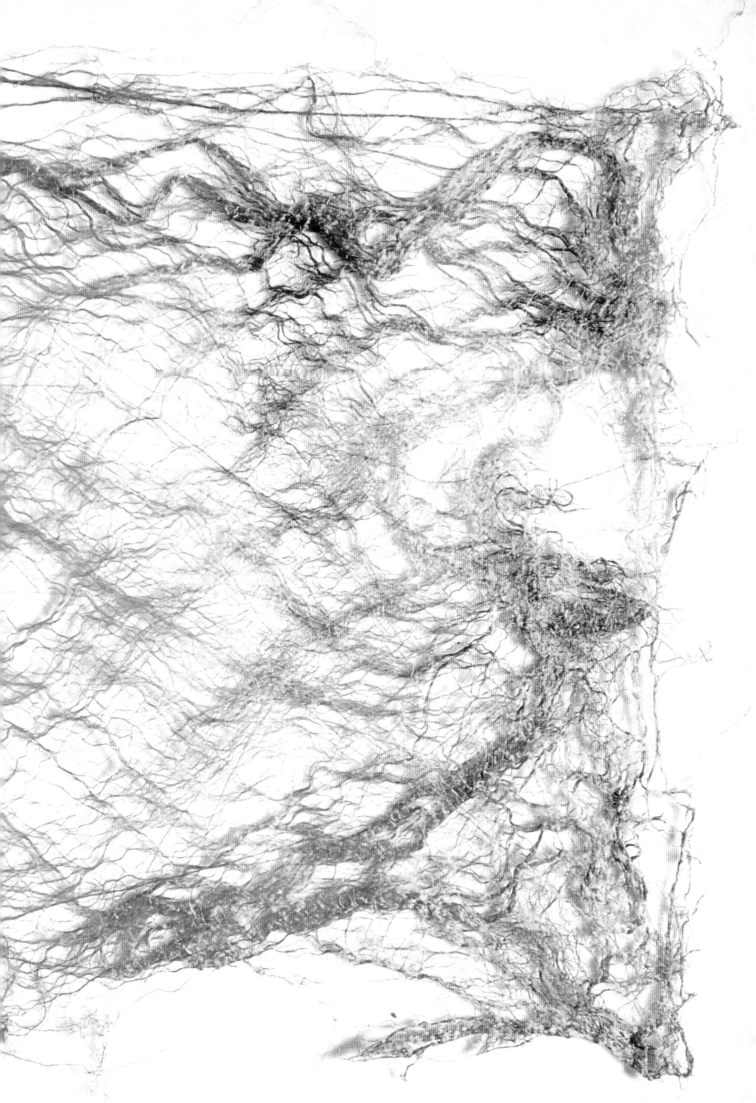

OTHER FIBRES

Fibres other than silk can also be made into paper using the basic techniques shown on pages 36–39. Raw jute, crimped jute, sisal and flax are stranded like throwster's waste. They can be used either dyed or undyed. Some of the other fibres are rather coarse, so you may find that you need a stronger concentration of paste. Alternatively, exploit the linear quality of these slivers to produce striped or woven papers.

As well as making interesting papers in their own right, natural fibres can also be used as a foundation for more delicate silk ones, to support them in a three-dimensional installation, perhaps.

Crimped jute and silk tops

These two fibres work very well together to create a delicate paper with a translucency that belies its strength. When building up a composite sheet, it is often easier to work with fibres of similar weight (or to marry pulled tufts of similar thickness). Wildly disparate fibres can tend to separate over time, unless a strong consistency of paste is used.

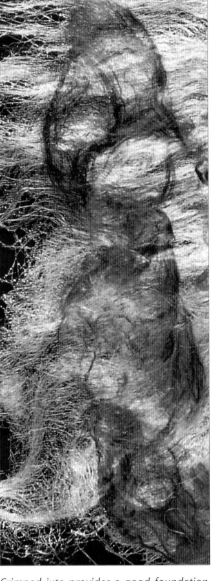

Crimped jute provides a good foundation for these delicate swirls of silk tops.

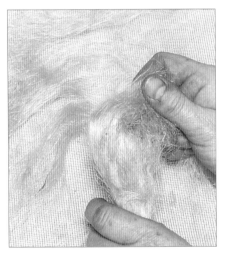

1. Separate the fibres from a hank of crimped jute and lay a fine bed of long fibres on the net.

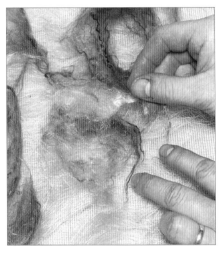

2. Pull long lengths of dyed silk tops and arrange them in swirls on top of the jute. Felt as shown on page 38. The finished paper is shown opposite, sitting on a sheet of silk noils paper.

Silk noils

Silk noils are the short, nubbly fibres taken from the inner part of silk cocoons. They are often used to make paper that is to act as a neutral foil for more exotic fibres or embellishments – as part of a multimedia project, for example. However, in their own right they have a rough, unkempt charm that is impossible to ignore.

Full-size detail from the sheet of silk noils paper shown opposite.

Opposite
The delicate sheet of paper made from crimped jute and dyed silk tops sits well on the solid, nubbly surface of a sheet of silk noils paper.

Woven flax

The joy of flax lies in its strength and versatility. Because it is commonly used in hand-spinning and weaving, it is readily available (but not particularly cheap). You can buy it in its natural state, bleached white or commercially dyed in a wide range of colours. For this project, I used ready-dyed flax slivers – long ribbons of fibre ideally suited to making a woven piece of paper.

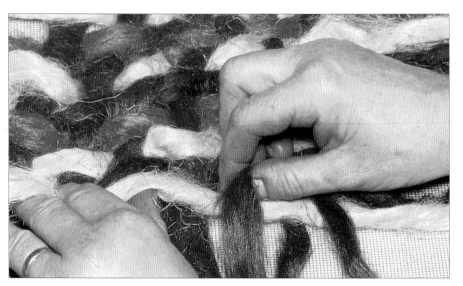

1. Lay down parallel slivers of flax on the felting net as a set of 'warp threads'. Each sliver should be approximately twice as long as the proposed sheet of paper.

2. Use other slivers of flax, in contrasting colourways, to form the 'weft threads'. Leave a generous margin at the top and then weave the first weft sliver under and over alternate warp threads. Weave more rows with other colours – remember to alternate the weaving on each row to create an interlocking grid.

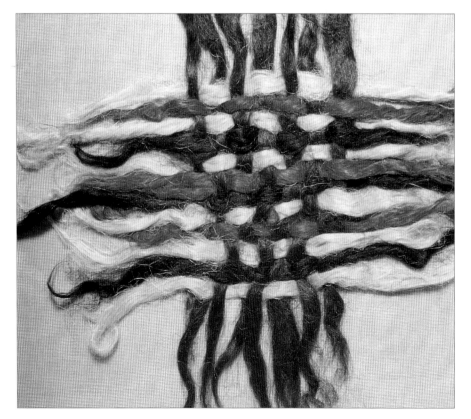

3. Continue weaving until the grid is the correct size. The result should be a wiggly weave of densely packed fibre. This fibre bed is quite thick so I suggest you dampen it with a water spray before felting in the normal way.

Alternatively you might consider using the felted fibres as the base for a three-dimensional vessel and mould it over a former as described on page 80. The long, unwoven warp and weft threads will spread out when wet, and these can be manipulated directly on the mould. Trim any ragged edges at the wet stage or when the moulding is dry.

The finished sheet of woven flax paper with the excess warp and weft threads trimmed off. Woven papers like this can be used as place mats or coasters. If you leave plenty of unwoven slivers unfelted, these can be raised into the vertical plane once the base is dry, much as you might make a woven basket from reeds, for example.

Raw jute

Unlike flax, jute fibres are coarse and are best treated as throwster's waste. Once felted, this paper is very strong relative to its weight, but you do need to use a double-strength adhesive to ensure long-term bonding between the fibres. These papers make a wonderful natural background 'trellis' for collages or stitching. They also make ideal screen panels and lampshades, particularly if backed with delicate, translucent mulberry tissues and then back-lit.

Raw jute fibres felted with a double-strength adhesive make this dramatic sheet of paper. Compare its texture with that of crimped jute shown on page 15.

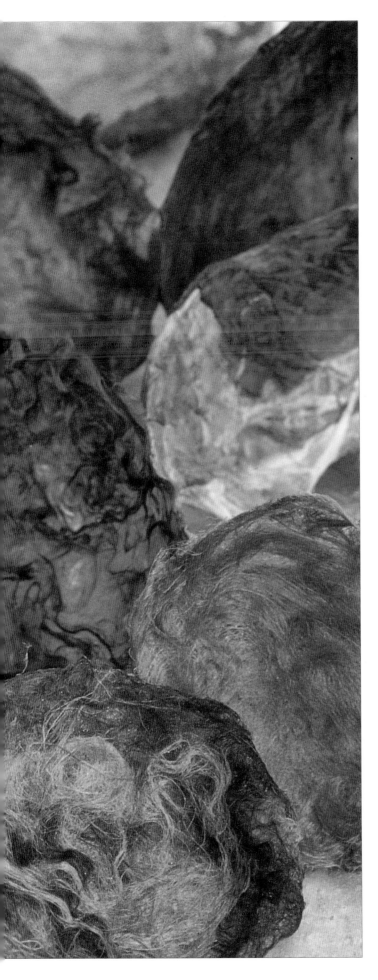

Moulding with silk papers

In its simplest form, moulding can be limited to manipulating the wet, felted fibres to create unusual shapes and textures on silk paper.

Silk fibres can also be used, in much the same way that you might use papier mâché, to create three-dimensional objects. For a first project I recommend that you choose a simple shape, such as a small bowl, on which to mould your sheet of paper. Remember that you must be able to remove the dried paper from the mould, so do not use anything that is rounder than a hemisphere. When you have mastered the basic techniques, you can then experiment with more complex shapes.

One important point, however, is that the adhesive used should be quite thick, perhaps double the normal strength, to give rigidity to the finished piece.

A collection of simple moulded vessels made from single layers of fibre, some with silk and others with natural fibres

MANIPULATING FIBRES

Silk fibres can be manipulated after the felting process to create stunning three-dimensional images with interesting shapes and lots of texture. In this example, I used undyed silk tops. Prepare a bed of silk fibres as shown on page 42, felt it and remove the top sheet of net. Place the felted fibres face down on a smooth flat surface as shown on page 48.

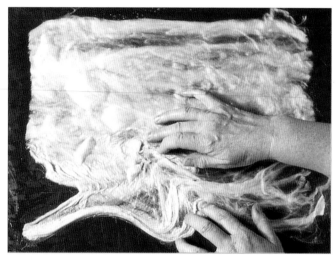

1. Remove the second net and start to manipulate the fibres – pushing, pulling and lifting them – to make an interesting design.

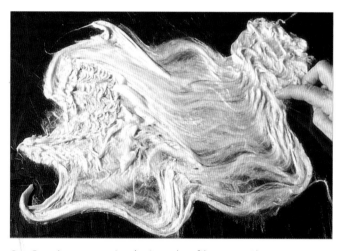

2. Continue manipulating the fibres until you are happy with the result, leave to dry and then use a flat blade to remove the moulded paper as shown on page 48.

The finished sheet of paper. This could now be painted or stitched, using the contours as a starting point for controlling the accent and intensity of colour. Notice that, although it started life as a rectangular bed of fibres, movement and interest have been enhanced by paying particular attention to the outer edges, and the asymmetrical balance of the sheet.

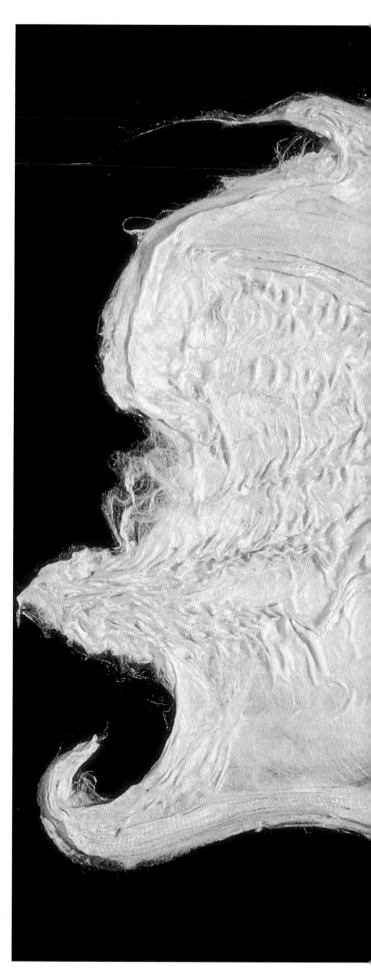

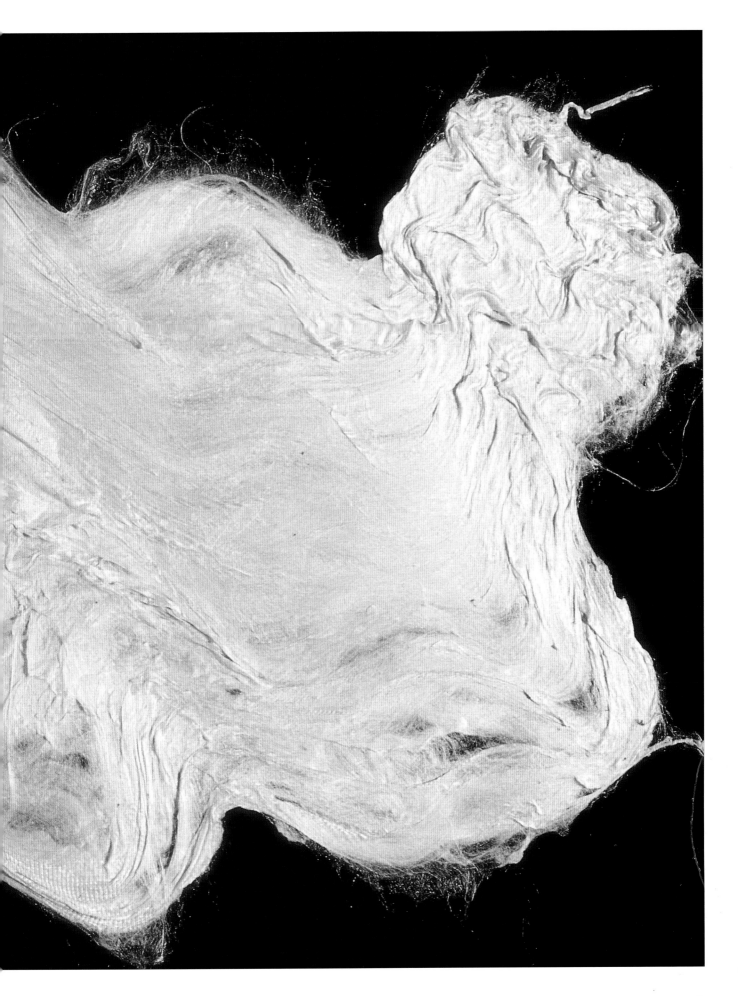

MAKING A SIMPLE BOWL

The shape that you choose for your former will obviously depend on the purpose to which the finished paper bowl is to be put. Here I have chosen to make a candle bowl, so it is important that the sides are steep and deep in order to protect the lit flame and its protective glass container from draughts. I have also chosen to laminate silk handkerchiefs on dyed tissue paper, felting them together on the mould.

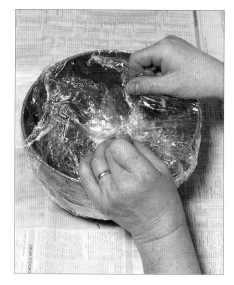

1. Cover the outside of the mould with cellulose kitchen wrap and tuck the excess ends down the inside.

2. Upturn the mould on a taller support, such as a sturdy bottle, to raise it off the work surface.

Moulding dry paper

You can also mould three-dimensional objects using pre-made, flat sheets of silk paper. To do this, soften the paper by spraying it with water and then apply the limp sheet to the mould. This technique is particularly useful when you want to embellish a three-dimensional object with embroidery, beads or other motifs. It is obviously much easier to apply embellishments to dry, flat sheets rather than moulded ones.

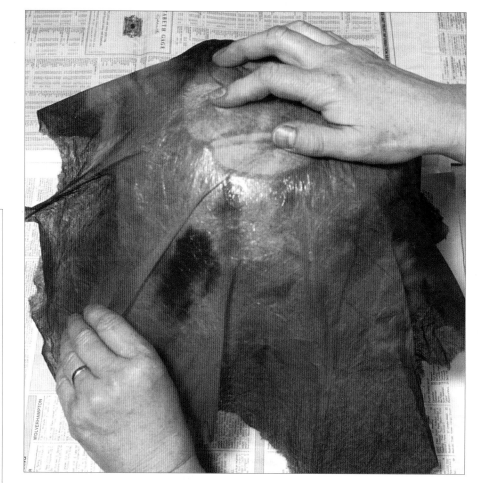

3. Lay a sheet of dyed tissue paper on the mould and then pleat the tissue to roughly fit the shape of the mould.

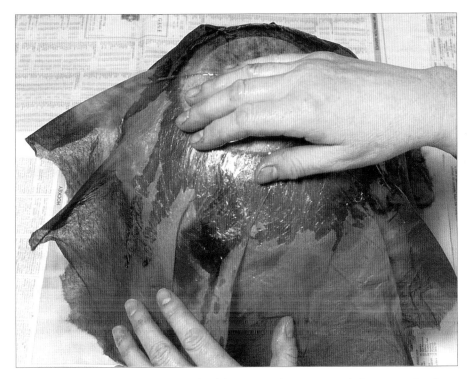

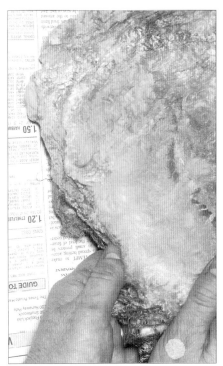

4. Wet the tissue with some double-strength paste and then manipulate the wet paper round the contours of the mould.

5. Separate a few layers from a dyed silk handkerchief.

6. Drape the silk handkerchief layers over the mould, allowing them to extend well down below the rim.

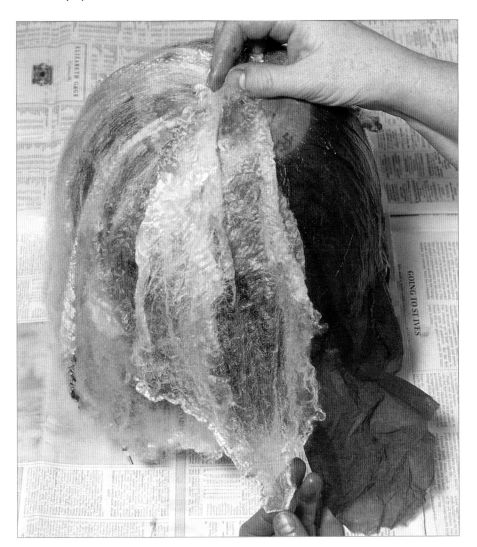

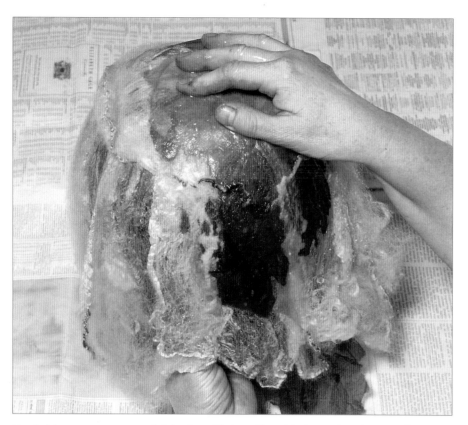

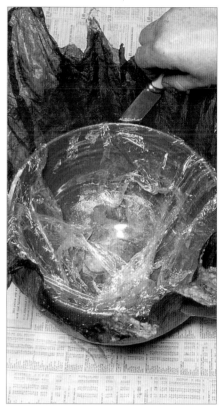

7. Add more paste and felt the silk handkerchiefs to the shape of the bowl. When all the fibres have been felted, leave to the bowl to dry.

8. Slide a flat-bladed knife around the rim of the mould and gently ease the paper from the sides of the mould.

9. When the paper is completely free, use the cellulose kitchen wrap to lift out the former.

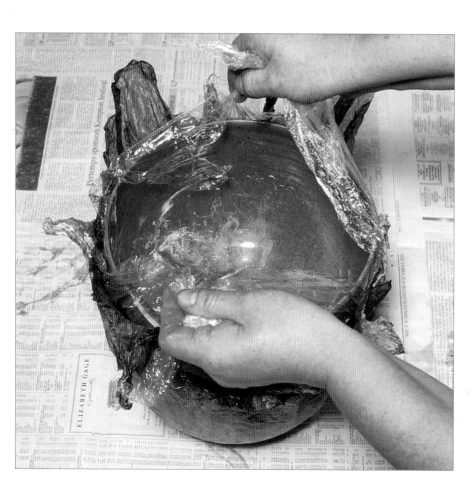

Opposite
The finished moulded bowl (top) together with a similar vessel in blue silk which has been edged and decorated with metallic bronze paint.

For a more formal edge to a bowl you can dampen the loose ends and turn them out to form a brim-shaped rim. Alternatively, trim them to size and/or turn them to the inside to create a straight rim.

Bowls can also be made from the other fibres mentioned in this book. Depending on the strength of the fibre and the adhesive paste, it is not always necessary to pre-line the mould with tissue. If you choose undyed fibres as your source material, you can decorate the finished vessel with paint or wax.

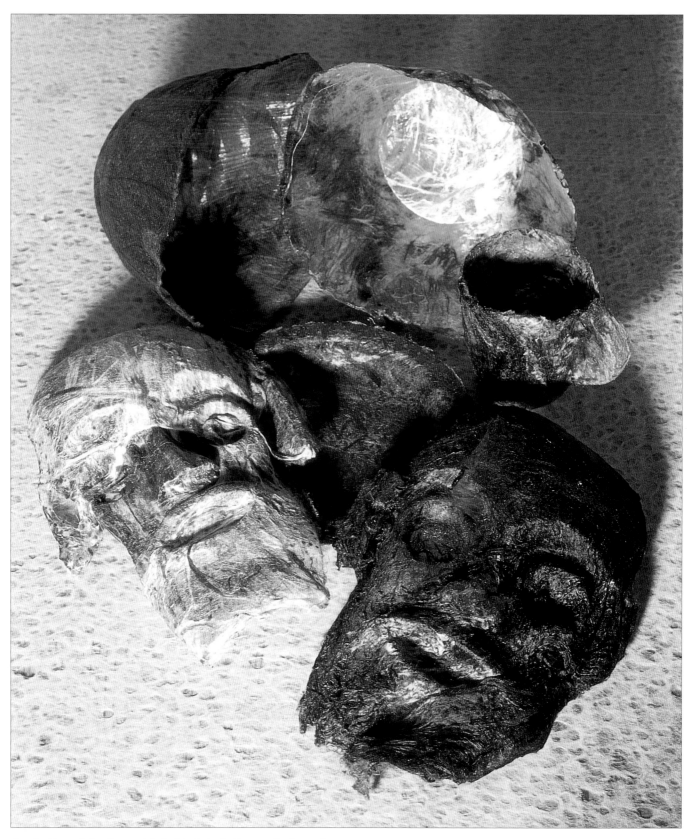

A collection of simple moulded objects including masks formed
on a wooden mould, a cup, a small plate and two bowls
moulded over ceramic and glass originals.

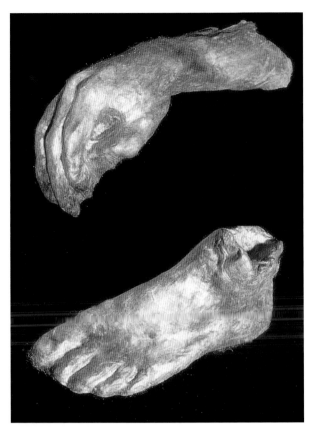

Silken casts by Diane Reade

Hand-dyed silk tops paper was cast over a modelled clay mould to produce these surreal casts.

Golden mask by Kath Russon

This mask is made by moulding natural flax inside a specially-made plaster of Paris mould. When dry, the mask was painted with gold acrylic paint.

Candle bowl by Kath Russon

Hanked filament paper was moulded over a ceramic planter, making a candle bowl which gently diffuses the light through the myriad of holes within the meshed framework.

MAKING SILK LEAVES

In the same way as you would make an impression of a coin or an inscription on a brass plate by rubbing, you can replicate leaves, keys, coins and other flat objects in silk paper, using a very easy embossing process. When they are dry, you can use the silk replicas to make earrings, to decorate two- and three-dimensional objects or to make birthday cards, gift tags or book covers.

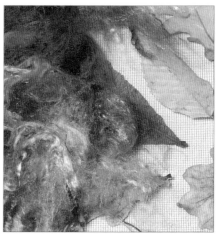

1. Gather together a collection of leaves and then sort them, discarding any with curled edges.

2. Arrange the flat leaves, vein side up, on a felting net, leaving small gaps between each one.

3. Cover the leaves with tufts of silk fibres, randomly overlapping colours and types of fibres.

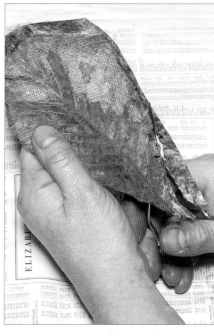

4. Cover the leaves with another net and then felt the silk fibres as shown on page 38. Leave to dry.

5. Rough cut the leaves from the dry sheet and then carefully cut round each leaf close to the edge. The natural leaf can now be removed and discarded.

A collection of silk leaves. Note how the veins in the natural leaves have been embossed into the silk fibres.

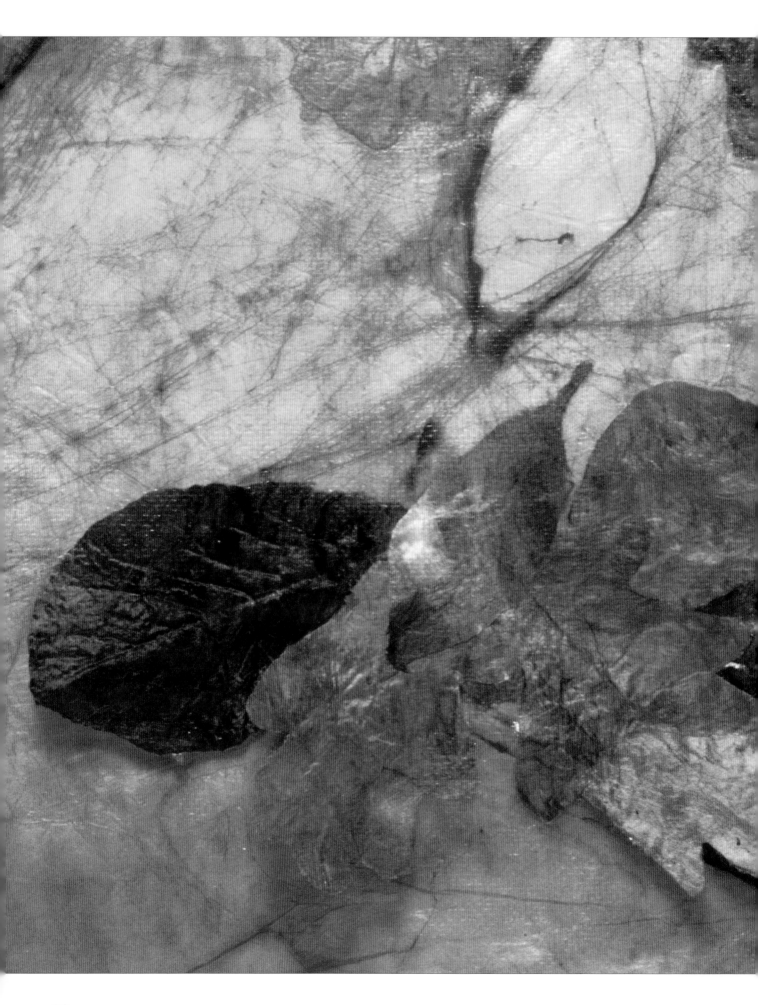

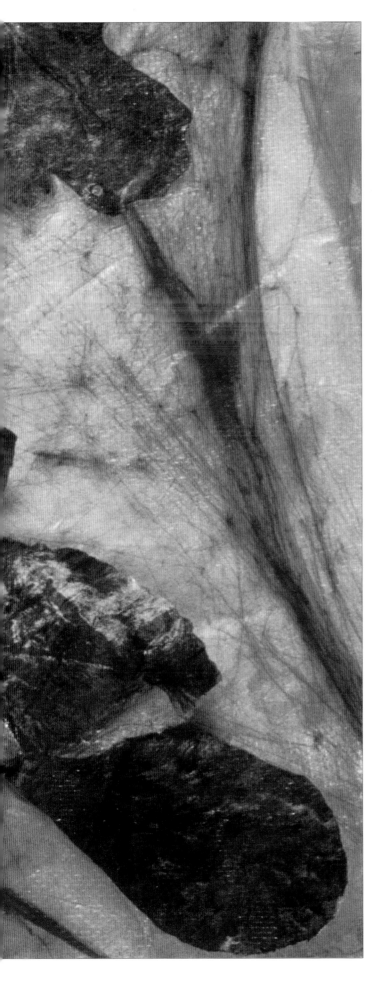

Using your silk paper

Silk paper is often used by embroiderers and textile artists as a foundation for stitching or for further collage. Sometimes it will stand alone and can be framed as an art form in its own right. It can also be used as wrapping for a special gift, as a cover for an artist's book or as the source material for decorated three-dimensional objects.

On the following pages I have included some beautiful finished collages, stitched items and more, to inspire you to create your own silk paper designs and finished objects.

Detail from the leaf collage on page 90.

Autumn collage by Kath Russon

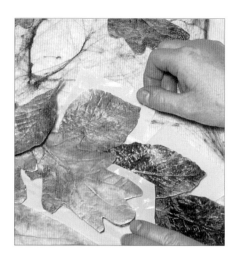

A sheet of silken tissue, hand-dyed in autumn shades, was made as described on page 58 and laid down as the background for this seasonal collage. Silk leaves, embossed from their natural counterparts as shown on page 86, were placed towards the top of the design and felted in the usual way.

However, I wanted the focal point of this collage to be the tumbled pile of fallen leaves in the foreground, so I used a slightly different technique for felting these. As each leaf was applied, it was separated from the background and other leaves by inserting scraps of heavy-duty plastic sheet under it. I was careful to ensure that every leaf retained a substantial point of contact with either the background tissue or another leaf.

When all the leaves were in place I felted them as normal. The scraps of plastic acted as resists and when the piece was dry they were removed. The free parts of each leaf were then dampened with water, moulded slightly and dried with a hair dryer. As a result, most of the leaves stand proud of the pile giving depth and realism to the finished collage.

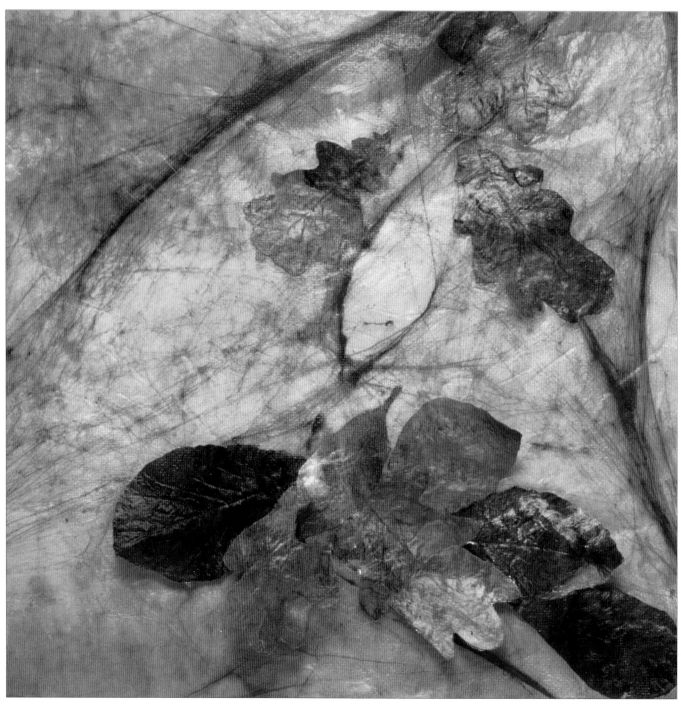

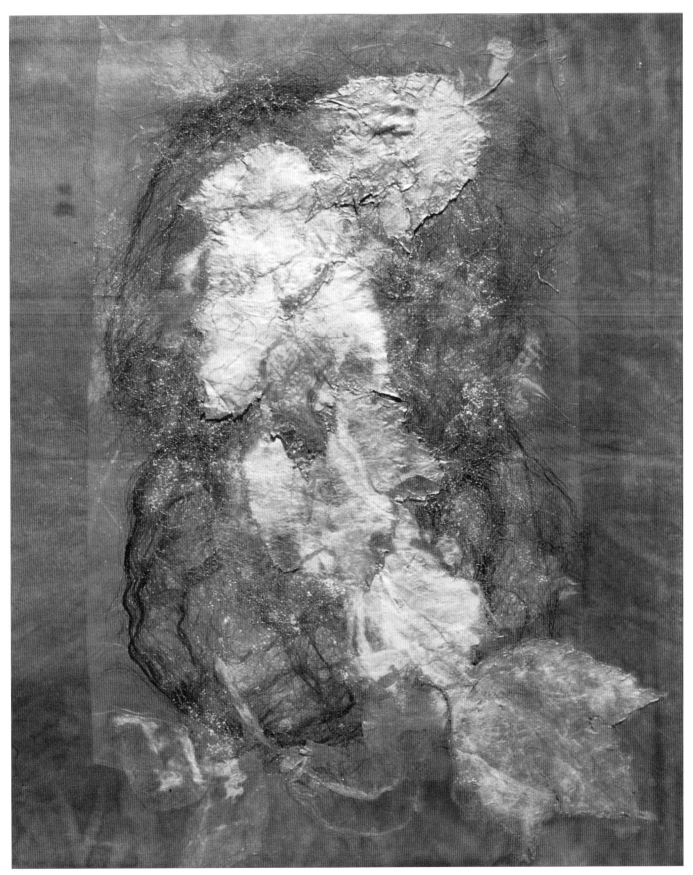

In contrast to the collage opposite, the leaf shapes in this composition form a flat focal point in a series of harmonious layers of fibres and silk papers. Dry gold metallic pigment was sponged on to the still-wet background fibres to illuminate their rough texture. When the complete design was dry, the veins and outer edges of the leaves were selectively highlighted with bronze metallic pigment.

Opposite
Fossil Layer by Maggie Grey.

*Drawn from a series of fossil studies, this design
has a silk paper base. The imagery is executed
using the computer-controlled Bernina Artista
180 machine, from a scanned image of fossils.
Fabric is manipulated together with further
layers of silk paper and stitch.*

Silken vessels by Niki Brown

*Niki used 410g (200lb) watercolour paper as a former for her
original designs. Unlike the moulds used on pages
80–85, these formers remain intact as part of the finished
pieces. As the pre-embellished or undecorated, silk paper was
applied, she took advantage of the wet adhesive to bend the
vessels into shape. The stab stitching was worked through holes
which had been pre-punched with an awl. The dangling beads
are strips of silk paper rolled into irregular cylindrical shapes.*

Silken book covers by Niki Brown and Kath Russon

Niki Brown's cover (top) is made from undyed silk tops paper, embellished with silk ribbons and embroidered with multicoloured pastel threads using a simple running stitch. The Japanese stab stitch binding echoes the embellishment. The other book is one of my creations. It has a hand-crafted paper cover which has been overlaid with a sheet of throwster's waste paper, hand-dyed in toning shades.

Opposite
Silken trinkets by Niki Brown

All the silk papers used here were first embroidered, decorated and beaded before being moulded over formers. As with the vessels shown on page 93, these formers remain intact as part of the finished pieces.

Index